The Eight Secrets

Of

Top Exam Performance In Law School

An Easy-To-Use, Step-By-Step Program For Achieving Great Grades!

By Charles H. Whitebread
The George T. Pfleger Professor of Law
University of Southern California

THE BAR/BRI GROUP

Previously published as *Success in Law School: Exam Taking Techniques.*

SUMMARY OF CONTENTS

Introduction: Handling the Intimidation Factor

The first year of law school challenges a student's intellect with a vigor and force rarely seen in American education. Professors try to sharpen the reasoning ability of students by showing them the limits of a particular principle and the relationship of legal principle to values. In an era of public concern for the teaching of values, legal education should pass muster from even the most value-oriented education critic. Because law orders our society, one cannot escape inquiry into what type of society will result from adoption of any particular legal principle or theory. Thus, first year law students must begin

1

to reason and "think like lawyers" while grappling with fundamental concepts of public policy.

The first year of legal education excites and involves students in a special way. The quality of the educational experience cannot be matched. Yet, no one would claim that the first year of law school is entirely pleasant or even comfortable. Part of the difficulty arises from the subtlety of the material and the magnitude of the educational goal which dramatically changes a student's way of looking at problems of everyday life. But many students don't simply find the first year experience demanding and challenging; they find it stressful and anxiety-producing.

Often students' anxiety is caused not by the intellectual enterprise but by what I call the "Intimidation Factor" of law school. At many law schools, the first year exudes intimidation. First, there is intimidation of students by some professors and then, every bit as commonly, there is substantial intimidation among the students themselves.

To show what I mean by the Intimidation Factor, take an example from my own law school career. The very first thing that greeted me upon entering the doors of law school was a large chart presenting the profile of my entering class by LSAT score. I had done quite well in undergraduate college but had not done so well on the LSAT. Imagine how I felt when I saw that they had had to extend the chart downward to include my less than stellar LSAT score.

Then came my first class, Civil Procedure. I was sitting in the back row, hoping for invisibility, the way so many novice law students do. A moment after the professor entered the classroom, he brought up a hypothetical case and then asked his first question, namely, "Who should decide this issue?" There were two choices—the judge or the jury. One large fellow sitting right in the front row began waving his hand furiously. The professor recognized him and here was the answer he gave to the question "Who should decide this issue?" "Twelve good persons tried and true drawn at random from the laity." I was so flabbergasted that I involuntarily gasped, "What did he say?" Well, not surprisingly, that student ended up near the **bottom** of the class, but on that first

2

day, I was so intimidated by his high blown response that I began to think of leaving law school.

The purpose of this book is to undercut and neutralize the Intimidation Factor of law school by giving you advice about techniques for success on law school examinations.

And, in case you haven't already realized it, success on your examinations is crucial—more important even than how well you answer orally in class. In most law schools, examination results dictate class standing, job opportunity, and access to the more prestigious extracurricular activities. This book presents a system that will enable you to maximize your scores on those all-important first year examinations.

Secret #1:
The Three Keys to Handling *Any* Essay Exam Question

T o be prepared for a law school examination, you must understand that there is a very real difference between what you are doing day to day in class and what you will be called upon to do on your examinations. In the first semester, you read and brief cases for class discussion. In class, professors ask you detailed questions about the cases assigned. If called on, you must know who the parties are, how they got to the court they are in, what is at stake, and even such details as which parties are from North Dakota. The focus day to day is your ability to read, brief, and analyze cases and statutes.

The focus of your examinations will be different. Law school exams assume your ability to read and brief a case. Thus, they test your understanding of legal principles by requiring you to analyze and apply those principles to hypothetical fact situations. This means that as exams approach, you do not want to study in ever finer detail the assigned cases; on the contrary, what you need for success on your examinations is the big picture of the course. You must understand and study the most significant legal issues in the course.

A word at this point about "legal issues" as I have styled them: These are not necessarily black letter rules of law. They may well be principles of public policy or even principles from other disciplines which the professor has brought to bear in discussing the ramifications of competing legal rules. Since law orders society in so many different ways, legal education draws more and more upon other disciplines to illuminate the policies underlying social and legal choice. Public policy issues and principles of other disciplines such as economics, history, philosophy, and the behavioral sciences may be far more important in your legal education than the pat black letter formulations nonlawyers associate with law. Thus, when I refer to understanding legal principles, I include these fundamental concepts of public policy as well. Indeed, you should be aware at the outset that often these "non-legal" issues are more significant for success on exams than knowing the black letter rules of your study outlines and headnotes.

So much depends on your examination results that you must prepare yourself mentally and perhaps even physically for the ordeal of first year exams. The sooner you begin looking beyond the minutiae of the casebook to organize your notes around the most important major issues of the course, the better off you will be as exams draw near. Nothing *impedes* maximizing your scores on law school exams so much as "that instinct for the capillaries," the obsession with smaller and smaller details at the expense of the big picture of the course. One look at the typical examination format will demonstrate my point.

THE EXAM

Several types of questions could appear on your examinations. Some professors pose objective questions—short True-False or multiple choice questions. Others draft the pure policy question such as "How does the doctrine of res ipsa loquitur act to allocate economic risk in American tort law?" Occasionally, you might get a take home examination or an open book examination. These types of exam questions will be discussed later in this book. (*See* Chapter IX.)

Most law professors seek to test your ability to perform the legal analysis that your clients will require of you. For that reason, the most common form of law school examination question presents a complex hypothetical set of facts and asks you to analyze the legal issues these facts raise. Essentially, the hypothetical fact pattern essay question presents a set of facts narrated in chronological order, about the way a client would present the problem to a lawyer. While there may be considerable variation, most hypothetical fact pattern essay questions are 200 to 500 words long and require you to analyze and understand the legal principles involved. For this reason the most important task is spotting the legal issues—that is, just seeing that these facts present one or more particular legal issues. If we assume, then, the traditional 200 to 500-word, hypothetical fact pattern essay question, there are three principal tasks you must perform *before* writing your answer:

1. Setting your time allocation—i.e., allocation of time among the questions (External Time Allocation), and allocation of time within your response to each question (Internal Time Allocation);
2. Reading the question and organizing the answer; and
3. Preparing to discuss each issue in an organized and concise manner.

The average student cracks open the exam, reads through the first question, and without further ado, writes an answer. If you do not wish to be an average (or below average) student, resist the temptation to follow that course. Instead, begin your exam with the three tasks above.

Secret #2: Adding Points to Your Score by Making Time Work *For You,* Not *Against* You

EXTERNAL TIME ALLOCATION

Students often criticize law school examinations for their immense time pressure. Frankly, attorneys often work under severe time constraints, as any student who clerks in a law office can attest. For that reason I think it is fundamentally fair to expect law students to respond quickly and cogently on examinations. But I am a law professor, and so naturally I defend the time pressure on law examinations.

Whether you are persuaded by my logic or not does not matter. You must be aware of the substantial time pressure on your exams so that you can take steps to deal with it before sitting for an examination.

9

The first task is in many ways the most important: time allocation. Many of your classmates will squander their time and fail to complete the exam. It is impossible to achieve a high mark on an exam you did not finish. Just completing the exam is the student's first and, in many cases, most formidable hurdle to success.

The first thing I advise you to do as soon as the exam is handed out is to make what I call the External Time Allocation—that is, the allocation of time among the questions on the exam. As soon as you are instructed to begin the exam, do *not* read the exam— just glance at it to determine how many questions there are, what their relative worth is, and how long you have to complete the exam. From this data assign a certain amount of the total time to each question. This is the all-important External Time Allocation. You should try to stick with your projected times religiously.

For illustration, assume three questions are on a three hour examination. All questions are entitled to the same amount of time *unless* some contrary instruction is given. If, for example, the examiner tells you questions one and two are worth 80% of the points on the exam, then these questions should be allocated 80% of the three hours available to complete the exam, and the third question should be allotted 20% of the three hours. But if I were any good at math, I would probably have gone to medical school, so let's postulate a very easy allocation: you have three hours to complete an exam with three questions all of equal value. What's the External Time Allocation? One hour for each question.

"What an insight!" you sneer. "You mean I've spent good money to have some guy tell me if there are three questions of equal value on a three hour exam, all are entitled to one hour! How dumb does he think I am?"

Believe it or not, there is no single thing more likely to improve your scores on law school examinations than to make the External Time Allocation and stick to it. To put it more negatively, there is no greater pitfall than to fail to make and abide by your External Time Allocation. If you write two hours on question one, you are effectively doomed on questions two and three.

Over the years I have heard several ingenious student explanations for failing to make and obey the External Time Allocation.

10

One of my favorites: "I wrote two hours on the first question because it was about a topic I know cold. I figured I could write the best answer in the class to question one in two hours. I'm sure the professor will remember the brilliance of my answer to the first question when she reads my less complete answers to questions two and three." Wrong. You cannot make up with a high score on question one what will be lost on the following questions, even if your answer to question one is brilliant. Let's consider why this technique fails you.

First, you are probably overwriting the answer if you take twice the amount of time you should have to produce it. Second, many professors take the attitude that other students could have discussed the issues in the first question in more detail had they taken two hours to do it. Third and most telling, many professors grade each question separately so they don't know what you wrote in answer to the first question when they are grading the other examination questions. There is, in other words, no "Halo Effect" from one question to another on law school exams.

Thus, you must make the External Time Allocation and be rigorous in adhering to it. That's easy to agree to as you calmly read this book while preparing for examinations. Talk is cheap when planning exam strategy, but once in the stressful environment of the exam room, many well-laid plans go awry. What you should do is make an appropriate External Time Allocation and observe your time limits. What if you meant to follow your External Time Allocation but in the heat of the examination you write one hour and a half on the first question, abridging your External Time Allocation? Can you be saved or is all hope of a good grade lost? Don't throw in the towel just yet. While you may not get the best grade on the exam, you can still have a presentable paper if you outline your answers to the final two questions rather than attempt complete essay answers. You must complete the exam in any event, and having exceeded your time limit on the first question, you should immediately plan to outline your answers to the remaining questions. For heaven's sake, don't waste more precious time wondering whether you should outline the remaining answers, just do it. Your outlines may not be as good as well-written essays but once you have written too long on

11

the first question, you really have no other choice. If your professor is primarily interested in your spotting the legal issues in a set of facts, you can get substantial credit or even full credit with a detailed well-organized outline of issues.

Outlining is a far better alternative than writing an hour and a half on the first question, an hour and a quarter on the second question and leaving fifteen minutes for the final question. Here is the kind of response most students give in fifteen minutes:

Question III

This question presents a lot of interesting and complex issues. I really could have said a great deal about this interesting question because I know a lot about these subjects but I'm all out of TIME.

Do not do this! Do not do what? Let's review.

First of all, you will avoid this time disaster because you will have made the External Time Allocation and will have adhered faithfully to it, allowing you to write three neat, well-organized essays. If somehow you have abridged the External Time Allocation on one question, you will outline your answers to the remaining questions so that you can present a completed exam.

Finally, even if you are so flustered under the pressures of taking the examination that you both violate the External Time Allocation and fail to outline, you still should not scrawl an excuse that includes the word "TIME" at the end of an incomplete answer. Why? No law professor was ever promoted or given a professional honor based on how he or she grades. Grading is a task that many law professors undertake reluctantly. For myself, I so enjoy teaching and so loathe grading exams that I often view my whole salary as paid solely to grade the exams. Only with each exam viewed this way can I survive the awesome grading process in large classes. Thus, you will have no sympathy from law professors like me for running out of time. The exam was designed specifically to test your ability to manage the time allotted to answer the questions. Furthermore, I teach Criminal Procedure and so do not believe in public confession. Do you see the point? Some examiners read exams so fast, they might not have noticed that you didn't finish had you not written "TIME" at the end of an incomplete question. Therefore, since there is nothing to be gained from writing "TIME" at the end of an answer you failed to complete, let the examiner figure out for himself or herself that you did not submit a full answer, and maybe, just maybe, it won't be noticed. Do not call attention to your weaknesses.

So, to review, the first crucial task—External Time Allocation—takes only a few seconds of exam time to perform but is the key to submitting a successful paper. Adhere to your time limits. If you find yourself with fifteen minutes left over at the end of the exam, you can go back to embellish your answers if you feel you still have more to say.

INTERNAL TIME ALLOCATION

The second time related task is Internal Time Allocation. How much time, space, and attention should you devote to each issue in an examination question? Ultimately, this cannot be decided until you have read the particular question and organized your answer. At this point I suggest two rules of thumb concerning Internal Time Allocation. These rules of thumb are not iron laws in the way the External Time Allocation is; furthermore, you will quickly see these rules of thumb for Internal Time Allocation often cut against each other.

The first general rule: larger and more significant issues in the course are presumptively entitled to more time, space, and attention in your answer than smaller ones. For example, in most torts courses the issue of legal duty or negligence outweighs the issue of damages, which many professors reach late in the course and discuss in a cursory way. In a torts essay, then, the presumption would be that the more significant and more discussed issue of negligence would be entitled to more time and space in your response than the less significant issue of damages.

Consider now the second rule of thumb about Internal Time Allocation and watch how it cuts against the first: The more debatable the particular issue seems in the question, the more time you should allot to it in your answer. Suppose your torts

13

professor asks a question in which someone rear-ends another car. In that case, there is little issue that the person who hit the automobile from the rear is likely to be liable; thus, the negligence issue is pretty cut and dried. The question goes on, however, to discuss at length how the parties were damaged. How much should you say about damages? Remember the second rule of thumb: The more debatable the issue is in the question, the more time and space it deserves on your essay. In this case, then, place more emphasis on the damages issue.

REVIEW

What have we done so far? As soon as you begin the examination, make the External Time Allocation. How long will this step take? Less than a minute, but there is nothing you can do so likely to improve your results on law school exams as to establish a rigid External Time Allocation. The first obstacle to your success is time pressure. All too many of your classmates will not finish their exams and so will get mediocre grades. You must finish your exam. There is no credit to be had for blank paper. Make the External Time Allocation and adhere to it.

If, under the stress of exam conditions, you abridge your time allocation, realize that your best bet is to outline your answers to the remaining questions. In any event, you must complete the examination to earn a good grade. The External Time Allocation can get you over the first hurdle to maximizing your scores on a law school examination.

As to Internal Time Allocation, there are two often competing rules of thumb: (1) larger issues in the course get more time and attention in your essay than smaller ones, and (2) the more debatable an issue in the question, the more time, space, and discussion you should allot it in your answer. Use these rules as guidelines to allot time among issues in a question.

Secret #3: Flawless Issue Spotting — The Crucial First Step For Top Exam Performance

At this point many people who teach examination skills would urge you to begin your ordeal by reading the entire exam. This is wrong. *Do not* read the whole test before you begin. Why not? Primarily because it wastes time. You already know about the considerable time pressure on law school exams. You do not have time to sit there reading the examination as if it were a newspaper. Therefore, I urge you to start with question one and answer the questions in the order in which they are presented.

Even if you could read all of the questions in less than one minute, it is still unwise to read the whole exam because it can cause **anxiety**. This probably happened to you at one time or another on your undergraduate exams. You read question one—just what you thought would be asked. Question two—easy. But, oh-oh! Question three—what on earth is that about? Your anxiety over question three may well poison your answers to the first two questions even though you know those topics well. So don't read the entire exam before you start; just go to the first question.

However, before you read the 200 to 500 words of the first hypothetical fact pattern, glance at the last two sentences of the question. There you will find what is known as the "call of the question"—what it is that your professor ultimately wants you to do with the facts you are about to read.

Why read the call of the question before reading the facts of the question? For one thing, knowing what you must do with the facts will improve your reading of the hypothetical. Secondly, the call of the question may narrow the issues. For example, if the professor asks, "What are the defendant's rights?" you can be sure that all the information about the plaintiff's rights, while interesting and even potentially relevant, is not central to your task. Sometimes too the call of the question tells you whether your professor wants a neutral analysis of the issues or wants you to advocate a particular position. Therefore, always find the call of the question before reading the hypothetical fact pattern essay question.

The call of the question resembles the punch line in a "shaggy dog story" type of joke. It pays to find out where you will be going before setting out. Failure to do so can be very costly. For instance, a few years ago on a performance bar examination, there was a question that presented eighty-five pages of material that concerned several parties and included court rules and complex cases on that ever popular civil procedure issue, certification of defendant classes in class action suits. So that the examinees

16

could complete the test within the time allotted, the examiners restricted the issues to only one party, one-third of the court rules, and one or two cases. The students who discovered the narrowing of the issues before they waded into the eighty-five pages of material passed the exam; those who did not read the limiting call of the question are probably still reading that stuff. Always find out what your destination is before you set out.

After checking the call of the question, slowly read the first question once through. Just read it. Do not begin circling words and drawing arrows. Just read the question. When you have finished, then go back and reread the question, and on this second run through, carefully examine the information presented—*i.e.,* question the question.

Most law professors pride themselves on how cleverly they draft hypothetical fact pattern essay questions. Since the examiner is limited to a few hundred words, almost all these questions are filled with legally relevant facts. So on the second reading, go from fact to fact, questioning each fact's relevance. For example, if, in a torts hypothetical, you are told that the principal actor is an off-duty police officer, ask yourself, "What is the relevance of that fact? Do off-duty police officers have some greater legal duty than ordinary citizens?" Question the question.

No sooner do I suggest that you question the question than I can foresee some of you overdoing it. For example, if, on the criminal law exam, the professor says the person is dead, do not question that. Don't wonder "Can we believe it? What if he weren't dead?" Don't get carried away here. Respect your professor's facts, and question only the relevance of those facts.

REVIEW

What have we done so far? First, glance at the call of the question. Next, slowly read the first question in its entirety, reading it through to get its general drift. Then reread the question with care. Be careful on this second reading. Examination hypothetical fact patterns are dense. Every sentence, every word, may have significance. On the second reading begin to pick out the legally relevant facts by questioning the question. Finally, a word

17

of caution! A few law professors use trivial trick questions, but most do not. Therefore, most facts are of some importance. You must evaluate their importance relative to the big picture. Attention to detail is a crucial asset for attorneys, but more important is the ability to see the major issues in the case. Thus, most professors do not try to trick you with small details but rather they want to see how you can perform with facts large and small as they appear for attorneys in a typical case. Thus, details are important, but developing principal issues and significant themes is far more important on law school examinations.

How much time have we consumed reading the question twice after glancing at the call of the question? If we assume a question of 200 to 500 words, even if you are a slow reader, you should be no more than 5 to 7 minutes into the one hour allotted to the first question, leaving you plenty of time for the tasks ahead.

Before we move to organize an answer, however, here is an opportunity for you to make a choice while taking the examination (a "choice point" as I call it). What have I urged you to do? Answer the questions one at a time, in order, beginning with the first question. If, however, after reading the first question twice, you feel lost or confused, leave it and begin the process again with question two. Answer question two and then go on to three. Finish with the first question. Do not sit and spin your wheels about the first question. Start with a question that you find easier.

The reason that you do not want to muck around on a question (sometimes for longer than your External Time Allocation), is that you may never write a good answer to that question and meanwhile you are upsetting your composure so that you do not present your best effort on the remaining questions, which may otherwise have been easy for you. My own experience suggests that passing over a question that troubles you has a second benefit. Once you have written pretty good answers to the other questions, and the exam jitters have abated, you can usually go back to the troubling question with a confidence that will oftentimes clear up your confusion. Sometimes, having some good answers finished helps you understand the point of the troublesome question and allows you to write an acceptable response.

This choice point raises a larger issue worth mentioning here.

There is a dramatic difference between the atmosphere in which you are reading this book and the atmosphere in an examination room. It is easy in the peace and calm of your own study room to promise yourself that you will use a particular exam strategy. It is quite another thing to stick with (or even remember) your strategy when you begin to get those hot flashes and cold sweats on the day of the exam. So I offer certain choices for you to make while you are taking the exam. The first: If you do not feel comfortable with the first question, immediately move on to the other questions and come back after you have written those answers.

With that said, let's move on to the next step in our method for success on your exams—organizing your answer.

Secret #4: Organizing Your Answer for Maximum Possible Points

fter you have read the question twice, questioning the question, organize the answer by making an outline of your response before beginning to write. The key to success on law school examinations is a well-organized presentation of what you know, and the key to a well-organized presentation is an outline.

In organizing, make a distinction between criminal law and torts examinations and all other exams. In criminal law and torts exams, hypothetical fact pattern essay questions usually present a

ransactions. In multiple transaction questions, initially
our answer *by transaction*. For example, on a torts
..., you might encounter the following fact pattern:

A's car hits B's car;
B skids off into C who stabs D;
E strikes A with his fists; and
All parties are poisoned to death at the hospital.

Organize initially by transaction:

A hits B, what issues?
B skids into C, what issues?
C stabs D, what issues?
E strikes A, what issues?
The poisoning, what issues?

Once you break a multiple transaction question into its components, you can then organize *each transaction* in the way you organize all other examination answers—*by legal issue*.

Thus, for torts and criminal law examination questions, watch for multiple transaction fact patterns. Once you spot multiple transaction fact patterns, isolate each transaction. Then organize each transaction *by legal issue*.

In contrast to criminal law and torts exams, other examinations usually present a chronological recitation of facts that are all part of a *single transaction*. In answering these single transaction hypotheticals, immediately organize chronologically *by legal issue*.

Consider the following example, which is considerably shorter and simpler than the hypothetical fact patterns you will most likely see on your examinations. Although this set of facts is easier than you should expect, the concepts of exam writing that I explain in organizing this fairly simple problem will be identical to those you use on more complex hypotheticals. Thus, I can teach the concepts from this simple problem; you can practice with more complex examples by doing the problems in the Appendix to this book as you prepare for your exams. No matter how complex the fact pattern of the question, use the same system of organization.

My example is from contracts:

> A makes an offer to B;
> B counters;
> A accepts;
> B fails to perform;
> None of this is in writing;
> A gets what remedy?

Here we have a series of incidents that compose a single transaction. Your answer to this question should be organized chronologically by legal issue.

What legal issues from contracts does this question present? Here, the facts point to the issues of offer and acceptance, breach of contract, the Statute of Frauds, and remedies:

Fact Pattern	Legal Issues
A makes an offer to B B counters A accepts	Offer and Acceptance
B fails to perform	Breach
None of this is in writing	Statute of Frauds
A gets what remedy?	Remedies

How do you know what legal issues a hypothetical fact pattern essay question involves? Where did the skeletal outline of our answer come from? It came from the single study aid that I urge you to make for every course—a one page checklist of the most significant issues in the course. This "major issues" checklist will contain only about eight to twelve entries, no more. You must memorize this checklist, and so you might consider some mnemonic device, such as making the first letters of the entries spell a familiar word. However you do it, you should make a single page, major issues checklist for every course and commit each checklist to memory.

In preparing for an examination, instead of studying ever smaller details, pull back from the minutiae and think about the course you have taken. What are the most important points the professor (or perhaps the author of the casebook or both) raised during this term? You can be virtually certain that these points, whether of law, public policy, or other disciplines, will be the focus of your examination.

The one page checklist of these major issues supplies the skeletal outline of your answer to a hypothetical fact pattern essay question. After you read the examination question, ask yourself, "Which of my major issues of the course arise in this set of facts?" Your organization by legal issue emerges from the one page outline of major issues in the course.

A typical one page, major issues checklist for contracts might look like this:

Contracts Major Issue Checklist

    I.   Offer and Acceptance—Formation of Contract

    II.   Rights and Obligations of Third Parties—Third Party Beneficiary Contracts

    III.   Assignment of Rights

    IV.   Terms of Contract—Actual terms—Parol Evidence Rule—Statute of Frauds

    V.   Performance of Contracts—Covenants, Conditions, and Duties

    VI.   Breach—Failure to Perform

    VII.   Remedies—Damages—Other Remedies

    VIII.   Quasi-Contract

Of these major issues, the ones that arise in our hypothetical are: offer and acceptance, breach, the Statute of Frauds, and remedies. The others aren't important to this question. Do you see how the basic outline of your response to a hypothetical fact pattern essay question is derived from the checklist of the major issues in the course? You just run through your checklist and consider the facts in light of checklist topics.

Once you have the main headings for a skeletal outline, you need to add subissues to flesh out your outline. For example, what are the subissues of the topic offer and acceptance? What is required to form a contract? As I recall, the requisites for making a contract are:

A. Legality of Object (you cannot contract to do something illegal, such as selling cocaine)
B. Capable Parties (you cannot contract with children or persons otherwise considered disabled from contracting)
C. Consideration
D. Assent

Several points about this suboutline of issues: First, where did these subheadings under offer and acceptance come from? From the other study aid that I suggest you make. For every entry on your major issues checklist, make a subchecklist of *components* of the major issue. So, for me, the components of the larger issue "offer and acceptance" were legality of object, capable parties, consideration, and assent. Thus, to outline your answer, you derive the skeletal outline from the major issues checklist; the more detailed outline comes from the checklist of component issues. So far, then, you have:

I. **Offer and Acceptance (Major issue)**
   A. Legality of Object ⎫ Checklist
   B. Capable Parties ⎬ of
   C. Consideration ⎬ Component
   D. Assent ⎭ Issues

From the major issues checklist and the component issues checklist, you will always be able to produce a basic outline of your answer to a hypothetical fact pattern essay question. Once again, with the component issues checklist, make sure you have a workable number of entries so that you can memorize the component issues for each entry on the major issues checklist. Normally you might expect an appropriate component issues checklist to contain no more than six entries.

Here are examples of component issue checklists for Breach, the Statute of Frauds, and Remedies.

Breach Component Issues Checklist

A. Maturing of Contract Duties
B. Discharge of Matured Contract Duty
    1. By Operation of Law
    2. By Subsequent Agreement of the Parties
    3. By Subsequent Unilateral Act of Obligee—Cancellation—Written Release
C. Impact of Breach on Aggrieved Party—"Minor" Breach vs. Material Breach
D. Duties of Aggrieved Party—Duty to Mitigate Damages

Statute of Frauds Component Issues Checklist

A. Defense to Contract—Failure to Comply with the Statute of Frauds
B. Exceptions That Take a Contract Out of the Statute of Frauds
    1. Part Performance
    2. Primary Promises
    3. U.C.C.—No Writing For Goods Under $500; Over $500 Requires a Writing Except:
        a. where manufacturer has begun production of special goods
        b. where goods delivered
        c. where payment received
        d. "goods" vs. "services"
    4. Contracts For Less Than One Year
C. What Constitutes a Writing?

Remedies Component Issue Checklist

A. Damages—Monetary Damages—must be certain
B. Specific Performance
C. Promissory Estoppel
D. Measure of Damages
E. Foreseeability
F. U.C.C. Remedies
   1. For Buyer
   2. For Seller

Second, you must tailor the system that I am presenting to your own professor and your own course. You aren't really taking the course "Contracts"; you are taking "Contracts from Professor X." Likewise, you aren't taking "Torts"; you are taking "Torts from Professor Y." If your law school class has multiple sections of the same course, you may have already noticed how much variation exists from professor to professor in the same subject. Often different sections use different books and begin and end on dissimilar topics even though the course has the same name. Few other education experiences contain such latitude of difference depending upon the professor's choices. For this system of exam taking to work for you, you must customize the general concepts to fit the particular course and professor you have.

More detail on tailoring the system to your own professor is discussed in Chapter VIII. To illustrate for now, suppose you read my component issues checklist for offer and acceptance and, seeing consideration among the subissues, you balk, thinking, "Wait a minute; my contracts professor taught consideration for nineteen weeks of the course. Consideration is on my major issues checklist." Fine, there is no problem. Do you see that the checklists must reflect your particular course? In a course where consideration was covered in just three class sessions, it ranks as a component of the larger issue of offer and acceptance or formation of contract, and as such it is on the component issues checklist. In other courses, in which the issue consideration got considerably more class time, consideration appropriately becomes an entry on the major issues checklist. Either way, you will discuss the issue of consideration in your answer to the hypothetical fact pattern we are analyzing.

Finally, as a glance at the "About the Author" note will show, I do not teach Contracts. I teach Criminal Procedure; Gifts, Wills and Trusts; and Children in the Legal System. All I recall about the law of contracts stems from my own first year course many (many) years ago. So if something I write about the substantive law of contracts does not jibe with what you have been learning, do not go into a dither. I am not trying to teach you contracts; I am teaching you a technique for writing law school examinations. Don't worry if some of what I say about contracts, in analyzing our paradigm question, does not agree with what you have been taught. The exam taking concepts are the focus here—not my discussion of the law of contracts.

REVIEW

How to organize the answer to hypothetical fact pattern essay questions: In multiple transaction fact patterns, break the facts down initially by transaction. Once you have separated the hypothetical into its component transactions, organize all hypothetical fact pattern essay questions by legal issue. You concoct a skeletal outline of issues by reference to your one page, major issues checklist. You add detail to your outline by including the entries on your component checklist for each large issue in your skeletal outline.

Before we examine a substantive method for actually answering hypothetical fact pattern essay questions, a word about my advice to organize multiple transaction questions first by transaction. Many students point out that dealing with the question transaction by transaction and discussing the legal issues within each transaction as I have advised can lead to repetition, because many of the same legal issues are raised in several of the transactions. Won't this involve too much time-consuming repetition? No, because you are free to incorporate your earlier analysis by reference if it is really identical. For example:

28

A hits B, what issues?

(1) Negligence—people who hit other motorists from
    the rear are usually liable.

B skids into C's car's rear end, what issues?

(1) Negligence—same principle as above.

Even if some repetition is involved, you are better off to repeat occasionally than to muddle the organization of your presentation. The initial division by transaction, followed by subsequent organization by legal issue, guarantees a well-organized response, which as I have said is essential to achieving a high score on your examination.

Finally, don't be so sure that similar issues from transaction to transaction really are the same. Often subtle differences in application arise in discussing the same legal issue in the factual context of two independent transactions. The organization that I suggest will help you to catch these nuances that may be necessary to see the subtle distinctions your professor has placed in the fact pattern and therefore to get a better grade.

Secret #5: The Hidden Traps to "IRAC" That Most Students Miss

Now we turn to the question of how to analyze a particular legal issue on a hypothetical fact pattern essay question. The technique is already familiar to many law students and usually goes under the acronym "IRAC."

First there is the "I"—*issue* recognition. This is crucial to your success on any examination. Many professors only want to know if you can identify the legal issues presented by a hypothetical fact pattern. For this reason, issue recognition is the most significant component of IRAC. Referring back to our contracts example in the last chapter, issue recognition would be identifying that the failure of B to perform raises a breach issue or that the lack of a writing evidencing the existence of a contract raises a Statute of Frauds issue.

Next comes the "R"—state the *rule* you believe applicable to the issue you have just spotted. Here for example: In certain circumstances, contracts must be in writing under the Statute of Frauds unless they come within a recognized exception to the writing requirement. The rule that you state may be a black letter legal principle *or* it may be a rule of public policy or of some related discipline such as economics. Some main points to remember here are that: (1) rules can and should be learned in advance of the exam, but (2) knowing a bunch of rules from a hornbook or outline will *not* get you a high grade on law school exams. Some of your classmates will learn all of the rules before the exam and regurgitate them in an unorganized and thoughtless way on the exam; they will get mediocre grades. The key to success is how well you organize your presentation of the rules you know and, as the next step in the IRAC system requires, how well you show the application of the rule to the question's set of facts.

The next step, the "A," is the *application* step which, along with issue recognition, is crucial to writing an outstanding paper. Whatever your rule, you must demonstrate with reference to the facts in the question how that rule applies. In our hypothetical, for example, you might say: We are told the contract was partly performed by A before B breached; therefore, this contract may fall within the part performance exception to the Statute of Frauds. You must, for a complete answer, apply the rule to the facts of the particular question.

Finally, there is the "C" of IRAC, the *conclusion*. Be sure to make your conclusionary remarks tentative and brief. In our example: The failure of this contract to be in writing is probably immaterial as it falls within an exception to the Statute of Frauds for part performance. A few words of caution about conclusions: (1) never be too conclusionary—leave yourself some room to explore other issues; and (2) never reach a conclusion without going through the other IRAC steps. In this latter regard, a law school examination is a bit like an old high school math test. You cannot get credit unless you show your "work," *i.e.*, how the conclusion was reached. The conclusion on a law school exam cannot be considered correct unless your discussion demonstrates why.

This, then, is the IRAC technique. Integrating IRAC for each debatable issue or heading of your skeletal outline gives you a final outline from which to write the answer. Again, no more than 15 to 20 minutes should be required to construct a well-organized final outline from which to write your response.

Let's do an example.

Suppose we IRAC the issue of consideration in our hypothetical contracts question:

1. *Issue:* Is there sufficient consideration to support this contract?

2. *Basic Rule:* (For our purposes, who cares what rule we select or even if the rule is correct under the law of contracts? Remember, I am not trying to teach you contracts; I am teaching a system of exam taking. At every point in our analysis do not worry about the accuracy of the rules stated; they serve only as examples of the IRAC technique.) The rule then: People have to give people something to support a contract.

3. *Application:* (Here again, possibly incorrect on the facts I have given, but for this illustration, assume neither A nor B seems to have supplied consideration sufficient to support a contract.) Application: Here, neither A nor B seems to have given anything (even a promise) to the other.

4. *Conclusion:* No just society would ever find a contract here because of the evident lack of consideration.

Wrong! Do not do what I just did in my conclusion—that is, reach such an absolutely positive, inflexible, one-sided conclusion. Why is this wrong? Well, first of all, your professor probably has drafted the facts so that they do not lend themselves to so clear a legal conclusion. Second, and perhaps just as important, when you make conclusionary assertions such as the one above you do not sound like an attorney. Firm assurances are exactly what your parents and other clients hope to hear when they consult an attorney. Clients want their attorneys to say, "Don't worry about a thing, sir or madam; no just society would ever find a contract on your set of facts." But that is not what attorneys tell their clients. What assessment do attorneys give? "Well, it could be this way; on the other hand, it could be that way." This ambivalence is one reason that your parents and other clients are often exasperated by an attorney's advice. So, when you write "No just society etc.," you do not sound like an attorney and your law school exam will suffer accordingly. Remember, there are mighty few attorneys in those big downtown office buildings assuring their clients "No just society etc."; so you shouldn't either. It is time you begin to sound like an attorney if you aspire to be one.

Let me make another crucial point about the dangers of being too conclusionary on hypothetical fact pattern essay questions. Each issue in a hypothetical must be resolved in a way that leads to the next. Put another way, you must never be so positive in your conclusion to a threshold issue that it obviates the need to discuss later issues. For example, on these facts there may or may not be a valid contract based on my analysis of offer and acceptance. If you are too firm in your conclusion that there is no consideration, the answer ends, because if there is definitely no consideration to support the contract, then there is no contract; and, if there is no contract, there is no need to discuss breach, the Statute of Frauds, or remedies since they are issues that presume the existence of a valid contract. Thus, you must resolve a debatable issue in a way that allows discussion of the next issue. For example: "It is debatable whether there is sufficient consideration to infer the existence of a valid contract. *But if there were* [the magic words] the next issue would be breach." Or continuing your answer: "B may not have breached this contract on my analysis, *but if he has*, he may have the defense of the Statute of Frauds," and so on down the line of issues.

As an aside, let me say that if you cannot moderate your conclusionary rhetoric, then modify our technique—make it "IRA," and don't reach any conclusions on the examination. Let your professor draw the conclusions. What do I mean? Well, let's do the issue of consideration again.

1. *Issue:* Is there sufficient consideration to support this contract?

2. ***Basic rule:*** People have to give people something to support a contract.
3. ***Application:*** Here, neither A nor B seems to have given anything (even a promise) to the other.

Then, stop here. Reach no conclusion at all. Move on to the next issue and let the reader reach the conclusion. Conclusions are not the key to success on law school exams. Spotting issues and applying whatever rules you assert to the facts your professor presents are the real skills that produce high grades.

Now if we put IRAC together with our outlines of the answer we should be ready to write our answer to the hypothetical fact pattern essay question. How does IRAC fit with our outlines? Let's take the topic of offer and acceptance as our example.

We took the major issue of offer and acceptance from the one page checklist of the major issues in your course—the source of the skeletal outline of an answer to a hypothetical fact pattern essay question. Next, the subissues of offer and acceptance make up the detailed outline of our answer. These subissues, you will recall, come from that second study aid you should prepare—the outline of component issues of each entry on the major issue checklist. In the case of offer and acceptance, the components we have been working with are: legality of object, capable parties, consideration, and assent. So our outline looks like this:

I. **Offer and Acceptance**
   A. Legality of Object
   B. Capable Parties
   C. Consideration
   D. Assent

Your answer should begin, "The first issue is offer and acceptance." At this point I advise you to state all the components of offer and acceptance. For example, "To create a valid contract, there must be legality of object, capable parties, consideration, and assent." (By the way, an option you might want to adopt is underlining any entry from your major issue and component issue checklists the first time that you refer to it in your answer to a

35

hypothetical fact pattern essay question. I would not underline the word or phrase more than once in any one answer, but underlining the word or phrase the very first time it appears may be useful to highlight your organization and display your knowledge, especially if the professor is primarily concerned with seeing that you spotted the relevant legal issues presented in the hypothetical. Underlining is up to you. It is an option you might consider, but it is not essential for success.) Why do I advise stating all the components of each major issue? Because you cannot get credit for blank space—that is, for issues not discussed. What if some issues, here legality of object and capable parties, do not seem debatable in your professor's facts. State all the components of offer and acceptance anyway in case (1) you are wrong in your belief that some component is nondebatable, or (2) the professor wants to see if you know the subissues of offer and acceptance. Assume that in our hypothetical fact pattern essay question the object of the contract is buying and selling baseball bats (a lawful object) and that both parties are businesspersons capable of contracting. You should state all the subissues or components of offer and acceptance, and then immediately dismiss the nondebatable ones, explaining why they seem nondebatable. For example:

> The first issue is offer and acceptance. To create a valid contract, there must be legality of object, capable parties, consideration, and assent. Here, there appears to be no issue of the legality of the object since the parties were contracting for the sale of baseball bats. Furthermore, since both parties are active businesspersons, there should be no question of the capacity of these parties to contract.

Thus, you have stated all the subissues or components, and then you have dismissed the nondebatable issues by application to the facts of your question. Again, do not be too firm in your conclusions. "It appears that" is preferable to "it is obvious that," "any fool can see," or other student favorites.

Once you dismiss the nondebatable issues by application to the facts in the question, you should IRAC the debatable issues. For instance:

> The first debatable issue seems to be whether there is sufficient consideration to support this contract. [Rule] People have to give people something to support a contract. [Application] Here, neither A nor B seems to have supplied sufficient consideration to support this contract. [Conclusion] Thus, there probably was insufficient consideration to support this contract. ***But if there were***, we need to analyze assent.

Then you need to IRAC the issue of assent in the same way. Again, at the risk of boring those who have the concept mastered, let's IRAC assent:

> The next issue is assent. [Rule] People have to nod their heads [I know it's silly, but so what?]. [Application] There was a lot of head nodding here; both A and B nodded early and often. [Conclusion] There was probably sufficient head nodding to constitute the required assent.

Move through the issues of breach, the Statute of Frauds, and remedies in just the same way.

All nonfrivolous issues merit discussion. Since your professor cannot give you any credit for issues never discussed, my own rule of thumb is: when in doubt, include it.

REVIEW

Use the IRAC technique to finish the outline you made using major and component issues. It is especially important for you to master the technique of moving from issue to issue on a hypothetical fact pattern essay question by arguing in the alternative, in the ***"but if there were"*** style. Being too conclusionary early in your answer, so that you eliminate the need to discuss subsequent issues in the question, can result in a failing exam. Discuss every debatable issue unless a particular issue has been removed from the question by the professor's examination instructions.

Secret #6:
Writing a Winning Exam Answer Every Time

How long has it taken you to read the question twice, produce a skeletal outline and a more detailed outline, and IRAC each debatable issue to produce the final outline? Usually this organizational and analytical phase should not require more than one-third of the time allotted for the hypothetical fact pattern essay question. If we assume for instance a one hour question, the organization and outlining should require 15 to 20 minutes, leaving you 40 to 45 minutes to write the response.

Have you wasted time with all this outlining, IRAC-ing, and analyzing? Most decidedly not. Time spent reading and organizing is well spent. As Professor Henry Weihofen has written:

> The novice, after doing his research, may be eager to get at his writing, without first digesting, organizing, and thinking through the implications of his material. But time spent in thinking, before you even start to prepare an outline, is time well spent. It may be the most worthwhile of all the time spent on the project. There is no more pathetic illusion than the trusting conviction that ideas will come, if we just start writing.*

The principal theme of this book is that organization is crucial to success on law school examinations. The paramount difference between "C" exams and "A" exams is not so much how many legal rules and principles the student has memorized, as how well organized is the presentation of what the student knows. Organization and cogent presentation are hallmarks of a first-rate law school exam. The more clearly you can demonstrate your organization the better. Every good examination displays its organization early in an answer and then follows that organization throughout the written response. Nearly all students will spot obvious issues and articulate some rules. Organization and application distinguish the top exams from the run of the mill exams; therefore, spending 15 to 20 minutes evolving a working outline of the answer is essential.

STARTING YOUR ANSWER

Because we have spent up to one-third of our precious time preparing to write a cogent, well-organized response, we do not have time to waste once we begin to write. Start with the first

---

*Henry Weihofen, *Legal Writing Style*, 135 (2d ed. 1980).

issue in your outline and pass from issue to issue as expeditiously as possible. There is no time for some of the silliness I have read in students' exams over the past twenty years. Don't waste time on what I call the "Big Windup"—statements such as, "There are many fascinating issues in the law of contracts and this question discusses a lot of them." Ridiculous. Skip the windup and go directly to the first issue. Another ludicrous Big Windup: "Contracts is a very complex but fascinating course containing complex and fascinating issues, several of which I particularly enjoyed studying and many of which are presented in this hypothetical question." This nonsense will get you nowhere, but will eat up time. Just begin: "The first issue is the issue of Offer and Acceptance," or even better: "The first issue is Offer and Acceptance."

Another waste of time comes from the student I call "the Historian." It appears that a large number of law students today were undergraduate history majors because there are a substantial number of students who cannot discuss anything without giving an unnecessary historical background for introduction. For example: "The first contract arose in Egypt and there have been contracts in every culture from then to now," or some such thing. Unless the course is legal history, or the professor has asked a question concerning the historical development of the particular issue, do not waste your time with historical buildup; proceed to the first topic in the outline as directly as you can. It may be interesting to learn that the Romans and Greeks had contracts but that fact is not germane to the question the professor asked.

So where do you start? Begin with the first topic, and then go from one issue to the next, in order, until you have covered all the topics of the outline. Say all you have to say about one issue before moving to the next. For example, you should write all your analysis of offer and acceptance before beginning the discussion of breach. If you think you might have more to say later about a topic but you are not sure, leave some space—some unused pages or part of a page in the answer book—between that topic and the next so you could return to that topic to write more if necessary. *Do not skip around from topic to topic.* Skipping back and forth from one topic to another undercuts the organization and diminishes the value of your answer.

To be sure you understand this point, suppose you begin your answer with offer and acceptance. You write seven or eight paragraphs on that topic, whatever it takes to cover legality of object, capable parties, consideration, and assent. Finish that discussion before beginning to analyze the next issue (breach). You must not mix topics—it produces the disorganization and confusion detrimental to success. So your answer should look structurally like this:

> O & A   (Offer and Acceptance)
> O & A
> O & A
> O & A
> O & A
> O & A
> O & A

Then,

> Breach
> Breach
> Breach

Never, never like this:

> O & A
> O & A
> O & A
> Breach
> O & A
> Breach
> Breach
> O & A
> O & A

Finish your discussion of one topic before proceeding to the next.

COPING DURING THE EXAM

What if halfway through your discussions of breach you realize that you have failed to discuss one-third of the relevant law of offer and acceptance? What should you do? *Not this:*

O & A
O & A
O & A
O & A
Breach
Breach
Oops! O & A
      O & A
      O & A

And note: this disastrous disorganization *cannot* be cured with the student's favorite palliative, the arrow:

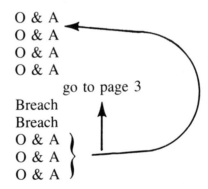

O & A
O & A
O & A
O & A
        go to page 3
Breach
Breach
O & A
O & A
O & A

The only place you will "go to" with that device is the middle of the class. *Do not do this.*

What can you do if midway through analyzing the issue of breach you suddenly discover that you forgot a segment of the law of the previous topic of offer and acceptance? The best solution is to go back and supplement your analysis of the previous topic in the blank space you left for further discussion between the first topic and the next. What if you did not leave any

43

space between offer and acceptance and breach? There is still a way to add the additional material in your examination book.

First, if you write your examination answers in blue books or other examination books, write on only one side of an examination book page. Use more exam books if necessary, but never write on both sides of a page. Why not? Well, for one thing, writing on both sides of the page makes your answer appear cramped, dense, and unpleasant to read. Second, if you use only one side of an examination book page, you will always have a blank facing page for every written page. Then you can use these blank facing pages, back where you were discussing the topic offer and acceptance, to add the material you left out.

So, if while you are discussing breach you realize that you have left something out of your discussion of offer and acceptance, go back in the examination book to the place where you were writing about that topic and put the addenda material on the blank facing page. Here, an arrow is proper; it should point across to the white facing page to guide the reader to the supplemental material.

Will adding this material on the facing page help? Yes. Although your professor will know this material came to you after your initial discussion of the topic, there is no sin in that, and you will not have destroyed your all-important organization. To be sure you understand my point:

Examination book:

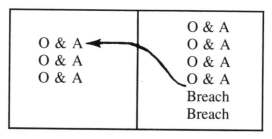

As corny as it may sound, this physical placement of the supplemental material with the topic it supplements can preserve the clarity and organization of your answer while allowing you to add the omitted material.

As I have mentioned, time is precious when writing your answer. Do not waste time copying facts, regurgitating facts, or copying authority; go immediately to the issues and refer to relevant facts only as you discuss each legal issue. If the question requires application of a court rule or statute, do not copy the whole rule or statute. Again, refer to relevant parts only as needed for analysis of any particular legal issue.

Two issues that seem to cause students special anxiety are how to use cases and other authority in exam answers and how to assume facts not presented in the hypothetical fact pattern essay question. By and large, you should *not* use case names in answering a hypothetical fact pattern essay question. Professors have no interest in your memorizing case names. Furthermore, if you get the names balled up or confused you may destroy an otherwise good answer. You must demonstrate your grasp of the legal principles and policies underlying the course materials; you do not need to know or use case names in your response.

If you do choose to use case names, all you need is a one name reference in parenthesis. For example. "There is an exception to the writing requirement of the Statute of Frauds for part performance (Grumbletiger) or (U.C.C. §704(a))." However, neither of these citations is really necessary, and there is even some downside risk if your references to authority are wrong. Therefore refer to authority sparingly and with caution.

There are two instances when I would *advise* you to refer to authority or cite case names. First, some cases are so famous that their names are a convenient shorthand for the legal issue itself. For example, it makes sense to say "The suspect was entitled to the *Miranda* warnings," rather than listing all the rights that the suspect has. *Miranda* is sufficiently well-known to refer to by name. (Indeed, as I have suggested to legions of students, if you don't know the *Miranda* case name, you must never watch television in America.)

Second, if the hypothetical you are discussing is based on a statute or rule that the professor has reproduced on the examination, then I would advise you to refer to it in abbreviated or shorthand form as authority for your assertions. If, for instance, the professor states the hypothetical is to be discussed within the

45

context of the following four sections of the Uniform Commercial Code, which are then reproduced for you, you should refer to the relevant section or subsections that serve as authority for your analysis. For example, "There is an exception to the writing requirement of the Statute of Frauds for part performance of the contract (U.C.C. §704(a))." In this case, reference to authority is helpful because it shows your professor that you can apply the given authority in your answer.

Now, what if there are facts that are essential to your analysis but which are not clearly presented in the question? How do you handle this problem? At the relevant point in your analysis, simply state what facts you are assuming and why they are relevant. Suppose in our contracts example that the question says nothing about whether there is a written document. You may state that since there is no direction on this point, your answer assumes that no such writing exists.

A word of caution: My own experience is that the novice is inclined to assume too many facts. Usually all the facts you need to support your analysis are contained in the question. If you feel the need to assume large numbers of unmentioned facts, you may well be discussing issues *not relevant* to the question. For example, in a Statute of Frauds discussion, if nothing is said about a writing the better method is simply to analyze the legal posture of the parties in the alternative. "If there is a writing, then . . . If there is no writing, then. . . ." Why assume anything? In similar fashion, any student who feels the need to assume facts about implied and quasi-contracts in our contracts example is certainly pursuing a red herring. There is no implied or quasi-contract issue in this question and the absence of the facts relevant to that issue should tip you off that the issue is just not covered in the hypothetical. Thus, do not assume too many facts. When you feel a great many potentially relevant and legally dispositive facts are missing from the question, you are probably pursuing an issue that does not properly fall within the ambit of the question.

Similarly, be sure to take the professor's exam as written. Do not rewrite the exam to ask questions you wish your professor had asked. For instance, you may consider yourself the class expert

46

on quasi-contracts. No one in the class knows more about that topic than you. Just wait until the professor sees how erudite you are in discussing the subtleties and nuances of quasi-contracts! Unfortunately for you, this contracts exam has no question about quasi-contracts. It is unbelievably frustrating, and so you want to work into your answer something about your specialty. Don't do it. All of us find it hard to resist showing off what we know. I myself was a great offender on this issue. My technique: "Although this set of facts does not appear to raise issues of quasi-contract, if it did . . ." (followed by all my outlines of quasi-contract). Try to resist this; it wastes time and does not get you any credit since you are discussing an issue *irrelevant* to the question the professor asked.

Another variant of the same problem is what I call the "Kitchen Sink Response." No matter what the question, the student simply reproduces all of his or her course outlines thinking "Here are all my course outlines; I don't know how they apply to this question, but I'll throw them in anyhow so that I can get as many points as possible." This is not a wise strategy. You won't get points for excess (irrelevant) information and you will probably lose points for all the clutter.

USING WINNING TECHNIQUES

First of all, write as clearly and legibly as you can. Anyone who has ever graded examinations can attest that grossly illegible papers create a veritable presumption of ineptitude. It is so unpleasant and taxing to read illegible responses that even the most judicious and fair-minded grader cannot help but resent the student who has produced such a sloppy mess and put the grader to so much unnecessary trouble. Furthermore, and much more significantly, sloppy, illegible exams give the appearance of disorganization, something that is always fatal on law school exams.

What should you do if you have poor penmanship? Either type or print your examination answers. What if you cannot type and do not have time to print? At least slow down and take as much care as you can to avoid your worst handwriting excesses. Even poor penmanship can be improved by slowing down, spreading out the words on the page, paragraphing frequently, and writing on only one side of a blue book page.

A word about typing exams: I strongly advise those who type well to do so. Why? A good, fast typist can produce a written product that is cleaner and usually more extensively analyzed than a comparable handwritten piece. It is a pleasure to read a well-typed exam, and the student typist can set forth his or her organization crisply and clearly. Finally, typing can be much faster than handwriting and so typists can develop their arguments more fully than handwriters. But there is a drawback to typing your exam. While typing does show off a good answer to its best advantage, typing also vividly reveals weaknesses. With a typed exam, missing analysis or improper application stands out starkly—every weakness is quickly evident. Typing then helps the good student but can hurt the mediocre one. Also, bad typing is worse than handwriting the exam. If you are only a marginal typist, do not type the exam. Typographical errors are like poor penmanship: they give the impression of confusion, sloppiness, and disorganization. Certainly no fledgling law student should try to learn to type mere days or weeks before the examination. Typing is a useful exam-taking skill, and might even be worth a summer school course before or during law school, but typists do not enjoy such an advantage on law school exams as to cause concern of fundamental unfairness in students who do not type. I cannot type and have found it no impediment in writing exams or scholarly papers and articles. Of course I wish I could type but have never felt so disadvantaged relative to typists that I have had to take time out to learn. (With the advent and spread of computers—especially for word processing—the typing skill is even more useful for all educated individuals. Maybe I'll break down and learn to type yet!)*

---

*The wave of the future here concerns the use of word processors and computers to take exams. At our school we permit students to do so. However, we do check the contents of the computers to make sure they do not contain impermissible information. At present many schools do not permit students to use computers but that should change radically in

This next technique for good exam writing may surprise many of you. Do not try to be cute or make jokes on law school examinations. No matter that your professor was consistently funny in class or that the exam questions are drafted in a witty or amusing way. No professor wants you to adopt a flippant or off-hand manner in writing the answers to the exam. Fundamentally, law school examinations are not funny: they are not funny for you to prepare for and take, and they are not funny for us to grade. Do not kid or joke around on these basically professional exercises. Make a lawyerlike, professional-styled, no nonsense presentation of what you have to say. It is quite remarkable to me how many students do not understand the dangers of clowning around on examinations. Don't do it.

While I advise a "lawyerlike" presentation, do not misunderstand me. You should not use the silly legalisms you have heard on television or elsewhere in writing your examination answers. Do not write: "The *said* contract was signed . . ."; "the *heretofore* letter"; "*the party of the first part* . . ."; or other legalese nonsense. Like many graders of exams, I am a great admirer of Professor Wydick's book *Plain English For Lawyers.*† Thus, another technique for receiving the maximum score on an exam is to write your answers in clear, cogent, simple English, and do not use legalisms or slang.

As to paragraphing, I have never really understood when one should paragraph—they always say a new paragraph for each new idea, but what does that mean? My only advice is paragraph frequently. Paragraphing breaks up the monolithic, heavy quality of writing and can show your organization more clearly. Whenever you think you might need a new paragraph, start one.

---

the near future. I believe schools might consider supplying their own computers for use in this way, thus avoiding the "impermissible information" problem altogether. In any event, I fervently believe students should be permitted the option of preparing examinations on computers and word processors.

† Richard C. Wydick, *Plain English for Lawyers* (Carolina Academic Press, 1985).

49

Finally, as I have said, do not write in big letters "TIME" at the end of an incomplete response indicating that you have run out of time to finish the answer. Why not? First, if you use the system I have presented, you will set and adhere to your External Time Allocation; therefore, you will always have time to write cogent answers to all questions on the exam.

But even if you abridge your External Time Allocation, you will present outlines in answer to the remaining questions; thus, you will have a complete response to all questions even if it is not fully written out. Finally, even if you are so hopeless that you abridge the External Time Allocation *and* forget to outline the answers to the remaining questions, you still should not red flag your ineptitude by scrawling "TIME" at the end of the question you did not have time to complete. Why not? For one thing, it will get you no sympathy or credit from the examiner. Your professor designed the exam precisely to see if you could allocate the allotted time in such a way as to complete the exam. The answer to that is quite apparent: *You could not*. Like legions of middling law students before you, you have failed the first task of a law school exam—namely, to complete it. That big "TIME" at the end of the incomplete response serves only to highlight your weakness. There is no credit to be had from confessing that you did not finish the examination. Don't call attention to your failure with that useless plea for sympathy, "TIME."

Secret #7:
Preparation—
The Detective Work
You Need to Do to
Determine What *Your*
Professor Will
Test On Your Exam

For the system I have presented in the earlier chapters to work for you, it cannot be my system; it has to be *your* system. To facilitate that transition, you must tailor the overall technique to the particular professor and course you have been taking.

As mentioned in Chapter V, I have no more significant insight than to remind you of what every law student discovers early in the first semester: You aren't taking "Torts"; you are taking "Torts from Professor X." You aren't taking "Contracts"; you are taking "Contracts from Professor Y." I do not know of any other academic enterprise with so much variation from section to section and teacher to teacher within a given course. Different sections of Torts or Contracts will commonly use different casebooks, highlight different topics, and concern different disciplines. One section of Torts or Contracts may be very economically oriented while another is not. One professor may spend three weeks on the issue of consideration while the other section's professor may gloss over the topic in two class sessions. For this reason it is up to you to tailor the overall system to the particular needs of your experience. You must discover prior to the exam what your professor finds especially significant and therefore likely to be covered on your exam.

How can you find out what your professor is most likely to test you on? There are three ways and you must use all these avenues if the system is going to work for you. First, ascertain what your professor writes about or is involved in. Past and present scholarly interest is an excellent guide to discovery of likely exam questions. Most law school professors do a great deal more than teach class. They are actively engaged in the scholarly tradition of the university. If your Contracts professor has written several articles on consideration and is now working on another, what do you think he is likely to ask on the exam? If the professor must read over and over again a discussion of some issue, it is a good bet that he will prefer an issue—in our example, consideration—that he finds intrinsically interesting.

In addition to writing interests and expertise, litigation interest may also provide an insight. If your professor is enmeshed in litigation about the part performance exception to the Statute of Frauds, expect something on that on the exam. Thus, the first clue to a professor's intellectual interests comes from analysis of his or her professional and scholarly interests.

A second effective guide is the amount of class time your particular professor devoted to any one issue. The general rule is the more class time devoted to an issue, the more likely it will appear on the examination. If, as we have hypothesized, one section of Contracts spent three weeks on consideration, while the other section dealt with the issue in just two class sessions, the first section is surely the more likely to find consideration tested

52

on their exam. There is one caveat here. Because professors in first year classes often spend a great deal of time at the beginning of the course just teaching students how to read and brief a case, there is a resulting tendency for early issues in the course to take inordinate amounts of class time. You will want to adjust a little for that natural and commonly encountered phenomenon. For instance, if seals and signatures for contracts was the first topic in your course, the professor's giving that topic two weeks of class is not as significant as spending two weeks of class on breach later in the course. Overall, however, the general rule holds: The more class time the professor gives an issue, the more likely it will show up on the exam.

The third and final way to uncover your professor's preferred examination topics is to read any available copies of that professor's past exams. Past exams are an excellent guide to the future. Many professors are far more innovative, inventive, and clever than I am about exam drafting. Still, I find there is ultimately only so much the professor can ask about on an exam. Thus, many of us give ourselves away on our past exams. A thorough analysis of your professor's past exams will surely show a pattern of which topics he or she finds more significant.

Again, let me be clear. This system can only work if you tailor the general model to the particularities of your professor and course. It is your job to employ the three techniques outlined above to fit the system to your needs.

Once you have an idea of what topics will be tested, how do you study? As you get closer and closer to the day of your examination, do not study and memorize more and more minutiae and detail. Instead, pull back from the material—the cases, rules, outlines—and think, "What are the three or four most significant issues or concepts my professor addressed this term?" These are the topics nearly certain to be covered on the examination. In this way you can be prepared in advance to discuss certain crucial ideas from the course. As I will declare several times in this chapter, you do not want to lose sight of the forest for the trees. Your success will hinge on displaying the depth of your understanding of the main concepts of the course. Too much fixation on detail can be very dangerous indeed.

53

Focus instead on the primary themes, policies, and ideas that underlie the material in the course. Memorizing more and more tiny insignificant points will obscure that crucial "Big Picture" of the course. You should concentrate your study on the most important themes and ideas.

Overall you need a well-developed plan of attack for each course and each examination. Ask yourself not only what are the most significant issues of this course, but *why* are they significant? You should learn the policies underlying the rules and understand the public policy perspective that informs the choice between competing rules. For example, what is it about economics risk allocation or about the functioning of a rational private choice economy that recommends the rule that a contract exists from the time the acceptance is mailed rather than from the time the acceptance is received by the offeror at his office? It will not do just to memorize the rule that there is a contract from the time the acceptance has been mailed. To be able to apply the rule in your examination question, you must think about why this rule is preferable to the alternative. Thus, the more you think about the social, political, or economic theory underlying the legal rules, the better your answer will be; not just because you can demonstrate that you understand public policy choices but also because your application of the rules will be far subtler and abler if you really do understand the public policy that underlies the particular legal principle.

It is precisely with these comments as background that I suggest that you not overdo memorization of rules in your study. Yes, there is a need to learn some rules, but all your classmates will buy outlines, hornbooks, and other compendia of rules in a desperate effort to cram as many rules into their heads as possible. However, that mindless, scattershot memorization approach is rarely successful. Why not? First, remember that the "R" of IRAC is not where the big grading returns are likely to be; spotting the legal issue and applying whatever rule you state to the facts the professor has given you are more important to success. Second, you will write a better examination if you understand the policy concepts that underlie legal principles. Mere memorization is not enough.

54

Having said that, I will concede that a good hornbook or outline can be very useful in preparing for law school exams. Well-written study guides can resolve and explain obscure areas if the professor or casebook is not clear. They will also address the public policy and social choices underpinning the various legal principles being discussed. Hornbooks and outlines are of course no substitute for class attendance, keying your studying to your particular professor's interests, and hard work; but they can eliminate the problem of having no idea what the relevant rules are in the particular field.

The central idea here is that the IRAC system, the rules and their exceptions, and the policy choices underlying the rules may be learned in advance of the exam. By the use of mnemonic devices and other memory aids, you can prepare in advance to know the body of law and theory likely to be relevant for answering hypothetical fact pattern essay questions on the exam. Checklists and other study aids suggested earlier in the book highlight those key areas of the course nearly certain to be covered on the exam. By judicious use of class notes, your casebook, and commercial hornbooks and outlines, you can prepare the "R" of IRAC in advance so that in the exam room you can concentrate on spotting the issues in the hypothetical fact pattern and applying the relevant rule to the facts of that question.

One other study tip: Do not fail to understand both sides of each major issue in the course; this is a common error among first year students. Do not think, as you consider a particular legal issue, "Any fool can see that B is trying to weasel out of her promised performance under this contract and no just society should permit her to get away with it." Passion may (or may not) have a place in the courtroom, but it has *no place* in studying for and writing law school exams.

Finally, as you study for your exams, *do not panic*. All you can expect of yourself is that you do your best on exams. Maintain your common sense, your sense of humor about yourself, and your perspective. As you get nearer to the day of the exam, please retain some sense of calm. You have far more to fear from panic in the face of all your outlines, notes, hornbooks, checklists, mnemonics, and the rest than you have to fear from lack of knowledge. If you have studied diligently, your greatest enemy on exams is not a lack of knowledge but panic. Don't worry; rather, keep in mind that no matter how little you know, there will be plenty of others taking that exam who know less.

Secret #8:
How to Crush Any Unusual Exam Your Professor Might Throw At You:

Open Book, Take Home, Multiple Choice, Short Answer, and Policy Questions

T hroughout this book, the primary focus has been the hypothetical fact pattern essay question, which is the classic style law school exam question. In the same way, we have assumed a closed book, no notes examination. However, at many schools today, open book and take home exams have begun to sprout up. Other styles of questions appear on exams as well, such as objective, short answer, and public policy discussion questions. This penultimate chapter discusses briefly those other possible exam and question styles.

OPEN BOOK AND TAKE HOME EXAMS

Perhaps the most important observation about these types of exams is that they are far more commonly encountered in second and third year law school courses than in first year courses. The overwhelming majority of first year law school examinations will be closed book, timed, in-school exams. It is in more advanced courses and seminars that the open book and take home exams flourish.

An open book examination is given in an examination room and is to be completed within a set time (usually the same length of time as a comparable closed book exam). The only difference from the classic closed book exam is that the professor will permit you to consult the casebook and your notes and study aids during the exam. Usually you may not consult commercial out-lines, noncourse books, or other students' notes. The concept of the open book exam, as I understand it, is to reduce the reward for sheer memorization and increase the reward for good analysis. But beware: My own experience both taking and occasionally (very rarely now) giving open book exams is that there is still a tremendous time pressure to complete the examination. The open book exam may lull you into thinking that you do not need to study or memorize anything before the exam because you can refer to your book and notes. The reality is that there is not time to do much consultation of notes if you hope to complete the examination. For this reason, I would advise you to study in roughly the same way for open book exams as for closed book examinations.

One advantage of the open book exam is that you can consult

your checklists during the exam in case you have forgotten some particular entry. But do not think that you can get away without checklists, study aids, and syntheses of the course material prior to the exam. You cannot sit thumbing through and reading portions of your notes or casebook and have any prayer of completing the exam.

My own experience suggests that open book exams are a bad idea for all parties concerned. Professors unconsciously tend to require more time-consuming work on open book exams on the theory that no prior memorization is required. In fact, the time pressure on open book exams is usually far greater than on comparable closed book exams. Thus, I advise you to study just as you would for a closed book exam. Keep in mind my motto as you prepare for an open book exam: "If you have to open that book during the exam, you are in trouble."

Very rarely professors will give the even less satisfactory and truly pernicious take home exam. Usually these exams are to be completed outside school (hence the name) and have some long time limit (*e.g.*, 24 to 28 hours). Because they cannot be proctored, take home exams are open book exams with little or no limitation on what you may consult. These exams are not really exams at all but far more closely resemble papers that must be prepared within a given time limit. Do not get wired on caffeine and write frantically for the full twenty-four hours! View these exams as short research papers. Spend a couple of hours preparing your outline of the topic of the exam. Often much of the authority you need is either supplied with the exam by the professor or is found on certain recommended pages of your class materials. After looking over the relevant material, follow the same basic procedure you used for the hypothetical fact pattern essay question: draw up a skeletal and ultimately more detailed outline of your paper (examination), and from this outline write a well-organized, cogent discussion. Do not write a long treatise— stick to the topic. Here again length is not nearly so important as the depth of analysis and the degree of organization in the presentation.

Many students try to use the whole take-home period to write some rambling, incoherent, desperate course synopsis. (I do not use take home exams and I pity any professor who does. What a lot of garbage that professor will be treated to as holiday or summer reading!) Again, treat the take home exam as the assignment of a short paper with limited research to be completed within a given time limit.

OBJECTIVE QUESTIONS

Because the Multistate Bar Examination uses a multiple choice format, and because other parts of some state bar exams use objective questions, more and more law professors include an objective part to their exams. Ease of grading may be another cause for the upsurge in objective questions, but that is probably just another student criticism of professors so common at exam time each year.

There are two main types of objective questions: true-false questions, in which you must determine whether a statement is true or false, and multiple choice questions, in which you have to decide which of several choices is the correct or at least "best" answer to the question.

For true-false questions, my two tentative recommendations to you are: (1) Read the question carefully, and do not answer until you understand what the assertion in the question says. (2) Your first impulse is overwhelmingly likely to be correct. On my own exams over the years (I used to ask objective questions but do not any longer), eighty-five percent of all changes on objective questions were from right to wrong. What do I mean when I tell you to stick with your first impulse? Let me give you an example: "Most trees are green. True or False?" (A badly drafted true-false question but so what; you are stuck with it.) How do you answer this? Trees are bare in winter and colorful in fall, and some trees have red or other colored leaves year round, but basically most trees are green most of the year. Therefore, this answer is true. Your first impulse was probably true; only deeper reflection caused you uncertainty and anxiety. Go with your first impulse. Yes, some professors will ask trick questions but on balance most won't; so go with your first impulse and do not dwell too long on any true-false question.

Multiple choice questions are far more common on law school exams than true-false questions, in part because the Multistate Bar Examination asks multiple choice questions. The keys to multiple choice questions are: (1) Read them carefully. Most give away their answer from reading. Fundamentally most multiple choice questions focus on reading comprehension as much as law. (2) You can gain a great advantage in answering multiple choice questions by using the process of elimination. If you use the process of elimination for all multiple choice questions on an exam, you will get many correct, not because you know the correct answer, but because you know that three of the four responses are incorrect or silly. Thus, you will get the same credit as the students who could identify the correct answer. The process of elimination takes a little longer, but in my experience these rewards justify the time involved. Again, I would advise you to stick with your first response and not overread the question.

To show you how to answer a multiple choice question, let's consider this example:

> Which of the following is most likely to be common law larceny?
> (a) Defendant took Jane's television set with the intent to return it the next day but dropped it and damaged it beyond repair.
> (b) Defendant took Jane's ring to wear to a ball, believing that the ring was glass. On discovering that the stone was a ruby, defendant failed to return the ring.
> (c) Mistakenly believing that larceny does not include the taking of animals, defendant took Jane's zebra and sold it.
> (d) Defendant trustee skimmed money out of Jane's trust fund to make donations to his law school.

By the way, common law larceny requires a wrongful taking or carrying away of the personal property of another without her consent and with the intent to permanently deprive her of her interest in the property. The intent to permanently deprive must exist at the time of the taking and defendant must take the property by trespass or trick. Defendant cannot have lawful possession for common law larceny. If defendant has lawful possession and engages in an illegal conversion, the common law crime is embezzlement, not larceny.

With that speedy primer of common law larceny as a background, think about choices (a) and (b). Both are incorrect because for common law larceny the intent to deprive permanently must exist at the time of the taking, not the case in (a) or (b). How about (d)? No, (d) is embezzlement; the trustee has lawful possession of the trust fund. For larceny the possession must be unlawful. What's the correct answer? (c). The question says defendant was mistaken in his belief that larceny did not include the taking of animals. Do not go behind that assertion. Yes, there is a body of common law suggesting that larceny could not include the taking of animals, but the examiner here has said that defendant was mistaken in that belief. You should take that assertion as correct. But even if you balk, notice how if you use the process of elimination, you know that (a), (b), and (d) are clearly wrong, leaving (c) as the correct response whether you know why or not.

Two points then: First, read multiple choice questions carefully but do not fixate on them. Your first impulse is quite likely correct and further nit-picking is only likely to muddy the water and send you haltingly from the correct answer to an incorrect one. Second, use the process of elimination and you will get a certain number of answers right just from spotting the incorrect responses and knowing the fourth response has to be right whether you can explain why or not.

One other point about multiple choice and true - false questions concerns the grading method. If your professor gives credit for all correct answers, answer all the questions. When unsure, make an educated guess; the process of elimination will help again here. If, however, your professor subtracts the number wrong from the number right, cut down on your guessing and leave any question that you don't have a fair hunch about unanswered. There is, I gather, a lively dispute among examiners as to which of these systems of grading objective questions produces the more accurate outcome. I have great friends—persuasive arguers—on both sides of the issue. Both the Multistate Bar Exam and I give credit for all correct answers. So much of my courtroom experience required educated guesswork, I prefer to reward it in my law students, but I certainly appreciate the opposite point of view. In any event, know how your professor will grade these questions and act accordingly.

SHORT ANSWER QUESTIONS

Some bar examinations and a fair number of law school exams now contain short answer questions designed to let you explain a concept, legal principle, or doctrine in a short space. For example, a professor might require you to identify and explain three of the following in one hour:

> common law larceny
> common law embezzlement
> common law robbery
> common law false pretenses

The first rule to remember with this type of question is use the time you are given. Don't just say, for example, that larceny is a crime against property and stop. If you have twenty minutes to discuss larceny, give the definition as I did above ("a wrongful taking or carrying away of the personal property of another . . ."), then maybe state an example of what would be and what would not be common law larceny, and maybe give other distinguishing features of the concept. The first danger is that you will literally "identify" the concept and stop. "Wow, is this easy," you're thinking. Wrong. Write a little 15 to 20 minute piece (use a couple of minutes to outline your answer before writing) on the topic. Extreme brevity is the greatest danger on short answer questions. Remember you cannot get credit for what is not there.

The second danger is disorganization of response. Use some of your time (up to one-fourth) to outline and organize as we did with the hypothetical fact pattern essay question so that your answer will be a clear and well-organized explanation of the topic. Please note that your organization time should be shorter than for a hypothetical. Why? Because in the hypothetical you had to spot the legal issues. With short answer or "identify" types of questions, the professor has usually told you what to write about, and so you can move directly to your outline.

The third danger with short answer questions is writing too much for too long, thereby abridging your External Time Allocation. Do not write 40 minutes on short answer questions designed for 20 minutes each. Allocate your time among the questions you must answer.

Again, what if you do write too long on the first short answer question? Use the same technique that you would use any time you violate the External Time Allocation. Outline your responses to the remaining short answer questions so that you can get back on schedule. Outlines are especially good substitutes for full written responses with short answer questions. The professor often wants to see if you understand the principle in question. You can use an outline to display that knowledge quite effectively. I'd be more inclined to outline short answer responses than responses to hypotheticals; so anytime you create a time bind, use outlines for the short answer responses.

Finally, with short answer questions, read the instructions carefully. (You probably don't need this advice, but I did.) If the professor asks, "Identify three of the following four" do not identify *all four* as I always did in the heat of panic. Read the directions calmly before you begin, so you know what it is you have to do.

POLICY QUESTIONS

Another style of exam question is what I call the "Big Policy Question." This question involves no issue spotting but instead requires a clear, cogent analysis of competing legal rules and public policy choices. A big policy question in Criminal Law might be:

Compare the Model Penal Code to the Federal Criminal Code to the existing state criminal statutes on larceny and larceny by trick.

Here rather than spotting the issue to write about, you should mix a discussion of the substantive rules from the three statutory schemes, while also discussing the policies underlying the competing definitions, to prepare a cogent, common sense analysis. You'd consider: What are the differences among the three codes? What examples do you have of different outcomes under the three definitions? What policy preferences recommend one definition or treatment over another and why? Organize your answer carefully and write as clearly as possible your analysis of the rules and their underlying policies.

The responses to these big policy questions can be anticipated in advance of the exam. If your professor or casebook, or both, use competing rules from different codes or other sources, consider the possibility of this style of question. A look at your professor's past exams will prove a useful and quick way to anticipate this style of question.

My colleagues in teaching law are sufficiently inventive and clever that I am certain there are several other types of questions they ask on exams that I am neither familiar with nor aware of, but I think we have dealt with what are surely the time-honored formats of law school exam questions. If faced with any other type of question, adapt the guidelines I have given in this book to the type of question you face, remembering that staying calm, organizing your analysis, and allotting your time wisely are keys to success.

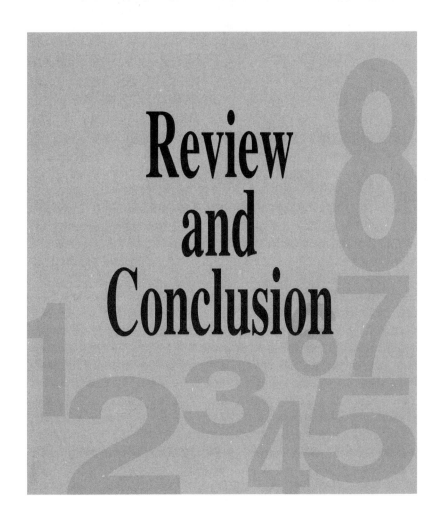

Review and Conclusion

To conclude, let's review the system that will help you to do your best on law school examinations.

I.   There are three principal tasks you must perform ***before*** writing your answer:
    A.   Setting your time allocation—External Time Allocation (among the questions) and Internal Time Allocation (allocation of time within your answer);

B.   Reading the question and skeletally organizing your answer; and

C.   Preparing a detailed outline of your answer.

II.   First, set the External Time Allocation; then glance at the call of the question in the first question.

III.   Next, read the first question twice. The second time you read it, question the question.

IV.   Organize first *by transaction* chronologically. Once you have the facts broken down by transaction, then organize always *by legal issue*.

V.   Make the skeletal outline from your major issues check-list. Produce the more detailed outline from your component issues checklist.

VI.   In writing your answer, state all the component issues of the major issue. Dismiss the nondebatable issues by application to the facts. IRAC the remaining debatable issues.

VII.   Write clearly and cogently, remembering that organization is crucial to success.

VIII. Do not panic. Panic, not lack of knowledge, is your worst enemy.

IX.   In studying for exams, *think*. Concentrate on the Big Picture of the course. Try to understand the policy underlying a legal rule; don't just memorize a lot of rules.

One last observation: No sooner will you pledge yourself to this system, which requires one-third of your time for organizing and outlining, then you will sit next to a person, who from the moment they hand out the exam, begins to write and write and write and write. The table or desk will shake frantically, his knee will pump up and down, and you may be spooked. There he is writing, writing, writing, and you are thinking, "I guess I'll IRAC; I should outline, but he's *writing*! Where is he getting it? Direct from God?"

No! Do not let this unnerving experience shake your game plan. Stick with the IRAC system. Take it from me; for twenty years I have been reading what that student has been writing, writing, writing. It's bilge, it's unorganized garbage, it's something like: "There are a lot of interesting contracts. There were some in Egypt, some in Rome. I even saw one last night on television. Let me tell you about that etc., etc., etc." I know that it is truly disconcerting to have the student next to you begin to write from the start. If this does happen to you (and my experience is that sooner or later it will), do not panic; do not abandon your organizing time. Just take a deep breath as the table shakes, lean back and think as you glance at this utterly flustered person, "That's one person I'm gonna beat for sure!" because with this system you will.

Appendix:

Sample Exam Questions and Model Answers

CRIMINAL LAW—CRIMINAL PROCEDURE

Sample Question Number 1

Police officers, believing Charlie's apartment to be a heroin distribution center, began surveillance of the apartment. Watching with the aid of binoculars from an apartment they had rented nearby, they observed the following events one night: Bart and Ned broke into Charlie's apartment and began to search it. Ned found a small box, which he placed in a briefcase he had brought with him when he entered. Charlie then entered the apartment. Ned shot Charlie, who returned the fire, killing Bart.

The watching officers apprehended Ned as he left the apartment carrying the briefcase. They seized the briefcase from Ned and forced the lock. The only object found in the briefcase was the box they had seen Ned place in the briefcase. The box contained heroin. When Charlie later surrendered himself at the police station, he was charged with possession of heroin. Ned was charged with four offenses: first degree murder, burglary, theft, and possession of heroin.

At the separate trials of Ned and Charlie, testimony of the foregoing events was received in evidence. The heroin found in the briefcase was received after appropriate motions to exclude it had been denied. The testimony of the police officers regarding their observations during surveillance of Charlie's apartment was also admitted over appropriate objections.

Based on the above evidence, Ned was convicted of first degree murder, burglary, theft, and possession of heroin, and Charlie was convicted of possession of heroin. Each has appealed.

What arguments should be made on behalf of Ned and on behalf of Charlie on each of their appeals, and how should the court rule on each argument? Discuss.

Answer to Sample Question Number 1

Criminal Procedure Part of Question

Step One: Divide the procedure part of the question by issue or party

71

1. Exclusion of the officers' testimony
2. Exclusion of the seized heroin

Exclusion of the Officers' Testimony

Step Two: Begin with the issue

The first constitutional issue that each defendant may raise is a claim that the police surveillance violated the Fourth Amendment prohibition against unreasonable searches and that, therefore, all evidence obtained as a result of the search should be excluded under the exclusionary rule.

Step Three: Set out the relevant rule of law

The Fourth Amendment to the United States Constitution prohibits unreasonable searches and seizures. Generally, for a search to be reasonable under the Fourth Amendment, it must be pursuant to a warrant. However, the Supreme Court has held that the Fourth Amendment will be violated only if the defendant had a reasonable expectation of privacy that was violated by the police conduct.

Step Four: Application

Here, the defendants each would argue that they had an expectation of privacy in Charlie's apartment and that that expectation of privacy was violated by the officers who were looking into Charlie's apartment with binoculars from a nearby apartment. Because the police did not obtain a warrant for this search, it was unconstitutional, and so the officers' testimony of what they observed should be excluded from evidence under the exclusionary rule. The exclusionary rule prohibits introduction of evidence obtained in violation of the Fourth Amendment and all other evidence derived from the unconstitutionally obtained evidence (*i.e.,* the *fruit of the poisonous tree doctrine*).

Step Five: Defenses

[Issue] At least as to Ned, the police will argue that he has no **standing** to object to the surveillance of Charlie's apartment. [Rule] To have standing to object to the legality of a search or seizure, the defendant must either own the premises or live there. Legitimate presence on the premises is a factor to be considered in an overall case-by-case analysis of the defendant's reasonable expectation of privacy, but here Ned broke into the apartment. Therefore, Ned was not legitimately on the premises and did not have standing to raise a Fourth Amendment claim.

[Application] As to Charlie, he is the owner of the apartment (leaseholder) and clearly has standing to object to the surveillance. However, the police may argue that there was no unconstitutional search here. Dicta in recent Supreme Court cases indicate that if the police observe things from a place where they are legally allowed to be, there is no search within the meaning of the Fourth Amendment, even if they are using a sense enhancing technological aid, at least when the sense enhancing technological aid is readily available to the public (*e.g.*, a pair of binoculars or a telephoto lens). On the other hand, the Supreme Court has noted that one has a strong expectation of privacy within one's home and obtaining information from within a home, at least when using sense enhancing technology that is not generally available to the public (*e.g.*, a thermal imager) constitutes a search.

Step Six: Conclusion

The warrantless search of Charlie's apartment clearly does not violate any of Ned's rights. Therefore, the officers' testimony against him cannot be excluded as fruit of the poisonous tree. Whether the warrantless search violated Charlie's Fourth Amendment rights is uncertain under current Supreme Court precedent. On the one hand, the Court might hold that there was no search because the officers were where they were legally allowed to be and were using commonly available technology (binoculars). On the other hand, the Court might hold that the expectation of privacy in the home is too strong to allow police to peer in with binoculars. Thus, it is uncertain whether the officers' testimony should be excluded as fruit of the poisonous tree in the case against Charlie.

Exclusion of the Seized Heroin

Step Two: Issue

The next constitutional issue is the legality of the search that produced the heroin.

Step Three: Rule of law

Incident to a lawful arrest, the police may search the person and areas into which that person might reach to destroy evidence or procure a weapon without the need of a warrant.

Step Four: Application

The seizure of the heroin is a valid warrantless seizure incident to a lawful arrest. Having observed Ned's breaking into Charlie's apartment and shooting Charlie, the police could validly arrest Ned. The police do not need a warrant to arrest a person who commits a felony in their presence.

Step Five: No defenses

Step Six: Conclusion

The court should rule that the heroin is admissible.

Criminal Law Part of Question

Step One: Divide the question by issue or crime

Ned: 1. First degree murder.
        2. Burglary
        3. Theft
        4. Possession of heroin

74

Charlie: 1. Possession of heroin

First degree murder

Step Two: Begin with issue

The issue is whether the court erred in finding Ned guilty of first degree murder.

Step Three: Set out the elements of the crime

First degree murder is the unlawful killing of a human with malice aforethought. Malice can be shown in four ways:
1. Intent to kill,
2. Intent to do serious bodily harm,

The depraved heart murder—wanton and willful acts creating serious danger, and Intent to commit a felony (felony murder).

Step Four: Application

Since Ned did not do the shooting that resulted in Bart's death, the state will likely rely on felony murder as the basis for this charge.

Step Five: Defense

Defendant can put forth the defense that he should not be held liable for the death of co-felon Bart as a result of resistance by the victim. This is the so-called *Redline* defense.

Step Six: Conclusion

If the jurisdiction recognizes the *Redline* defense, Ned is not guilty of first degree murder.

Burglary

Step Two: Issue

The next issue is whether the court erred in finding Ned guilty of burglary.

Step Three: Rule of law

Burglary is the breaking and entering the dwelling house of another with intent to commit a felony inside.

Step Four: Application

Ned's conduct fits all of the burglary elements if he had the intent to commit the felony inside Charlie's apartment at the time of the breaking and entering.

Step Five: Defenses

Ned can claim that he had no intent to commit a felony when he broke into Charlie's apartment, but this argument will fail.

Step Six: Conclusion

Ned has been properly convicted of burglary.

Theft

Step Two: Issue

The next issue is whether the court erred in finding Ned guilty of theft.

Step Three: Rule of law

The elements of theft are:

1. Trespassory or wrongful
2. Taking or carrying away of
3. Personal property
4. Of another
5. With intent permanently to deprive

Step Four: Application

Ned meets all the elements of theft.

Step Five: No defenses

Step Six: Conclusion

Ned has properly been convicted of theft.

Possession of Heroin—Ned

Step Two: Issue

The next issue is whether the court erred in finding Ned guilty of possession of heroin.

Step Three: Rule of law

Possession is almost a strict liability offense; basically, all that is required is possession of the heroin.

Step Four: Application

Ned had possession of the heroin.

Step Five: No defenses

Step Six: Conclusion

Ned has properly been found guilty of possession of heroin.

Possession of Heroin—Charlie

Step Two: Issue

Charlie can be convicted of possession of heroin if the jury believes the testimony of the officers who observed his apartment. The key issue for Charlie is the procedural objection to the officers' testimony (discussed above). If the testimony is admitted, the jury can find Charlie guilty of possession of heroin.

WILLS & TRUSTS

Sample Question Number 2

On March 1, 1986, Alfred validly executed a will that contained the following provisions:

1) I give my government bonds to Y charity;
2) I give ten percent of the balance of my estate to my nephew, John, on the condition that he is still married at the time of my death to his present wife, Kathleen;
3) I give the residue of my estate not passing to John to my niece, Barbara.

On March 20, 1987, Alfred sent the following handwritten letter to Barbara:

I have established a trust for your children at the A Bank. This trust should be worth approximately $50,000 and is composed of all of my U.S. and State X bonds. I am sure you will be able to decide how these funds should be used.

This is the only document evidencing Alfred's intention to establish a trust. Barbara's two children, Carol and David, were then adults.

On March 1, 1986, when Alfred wrote his will, he owned U.S. bonds worth $20,000, State X bonds worth $30,000, and State Z bonds worth $50,000. When Alfred died in 1989, all of these bonds were still registered in his name and had never been out of his possession.

In 1988, John and Kathleen were divorced. At his death in 1989, Alfred was unmarried and was survived by John, who had no children, Barbara, and Barbara's two children, Carol and David.

1. What are the rights of John, Barbara, and Barbara's children? Discuss.

2. If the court finds a valid trust created by the letter of March 20, 1987, what are the rights of the Y charity? Discuss.

Answer to Sample Question Number 2

Step One: Spot the issues and divide your analysis by issue

1. Validity of Trust
   a. Elements of a valid trust
   b. Delivery of a trust res
2. Holographic Codicil—Testamentary Trust
3. Ademption
4. Conditional Gift

Validity of Trust

Step Two: Begin with the issue

The first issue is the **validity of the inter vivos trust.**

Step Three: Set out the relevant rule of law

A valid trust requires: (1) an intent by the settlor to create a trust, (2) identifiable beneficiaries (for a private trust), (3) a presently existing trust res, (4) delivery of the trust res if settlor is not himself trustee, and (5) a writing in the case of trusts of land as required by the Statute of Frauds.

Step Four: Application

A trust requires no formalities for its creation; thus Alfred's letter is sufficient as it shows Alfred's clear intent to create a trust. The second element of a trust is met: the beneficiaries are ascertained (B's children). There is a trust res, the bonds. The main difficulty here is the lack of delivery of the trust res. Alfred has merely sent a letter but has not delivered any of the bonds. Delivery is required if another is to be a trustee.

Step Five: Defenses

If Alfred (the settlor) meant for himself to be trustee (the so-called declaration of trust), then no delivery of the trust res is required. Since Alfred did not expressly name a trustee, it could be argued that he meant to act as trustee. However, this interpretation is not convincing. His letter suggests that he intended Barbara to act as trustee since he states that she "will be able to decide how these funds should be used." Thus, delivery would be required.

Alfred's letter might be construed as creating a testamentary trust, in which case no delivery of the trust res is required until the settlor's death. However, for this to be a testamentary trust, the letter would have to be a will or codicil; see the discussion below.

Step Six: Conclusion

The trust will probably fail due to lack of delivery.

Holographic Will or Codicil—Testamentary Trust

Step Two: Issue

The next issue is whether the letter is a ***holographic will or codicil.***

Step Three: Rule of law

To be a valid holographic will or codicil, the signature and material provisions of the document must be in the handwriting of the testator, and the testator must have intended the writing to be a will or codicil.

Step Four: Application

Here one could argue that the March 20 letter to Barbara was a holographic codicil to Alfred's March 1 will. Holographs can be codicils to formal wills.

If the letter is seen as a holographic codicil, it would support the claim that by the letter Alfred has created a testamentary trust, which would excuse nondelivery of the trust res (the bonds).

Step Five: Defenses

The real issue here is a debatable question of whether Alfred had the requisite **intent** to make the March 20 letter a codicil to his will. Intent would be crucial. If Alfred had no such intent, the letter will not be a codicil creating a testamentary trust. There is no indication here that Alfred intended the letter to be a codicil.

Step Six: Conclusion

The letter is probably not a holographic codicil to Alfred's will because he did not intend it as such.

Conditional Gift to John

Step Two: Issue

The next issue is the effect of John's divorce on the condition of his gift.

Step Three: Rule of law

Illegal conditions or those contrary to public policy may be struck from a will. Otherwise, failure to meet the required condition will cause the legatee's gift to fail.

Step Four: Application

The condition that John still be married to his first wife is neither illegal nor contrary to public policy, and so his divorce means that his gift fails and should pass to Barbara, the residuary legatee.

Step Five: Defenses

John can try to argue the condition is contrary to public policy. This argument is weak; although conditions attempting to prevent or end marriages are generally considered to be against public policy, a condition to encourage a marriage is most likely valid.

Step Six: Conclusion

Barbara will likely take John's gift.

Ademption

Step Two: Issue

If the letter is a holographic codicil, the next issue, is one of *ademption.*

Step Three: Rule of law

When the subject matter of a specific bequest is not found, at probate, to be within the decedent's estate, that gift is "adeemed" and the legatee gets nothing.

Steps Four and Five: Application, Defenses

Today courts have tried to avoid the rigors of the doctrine of ademption by construing many legacies as general rather than specific. If the government bonds are construed as a specific bequest and not found in the estate, the legacy is adeemed. If the gift of the bonds is seen to be a general bequest, the Y charity gets the money value of the bonds and its legacy is not adeemed.

Step Six: Conclusion

The U.S. and State X bonds belong to Barbara's children pursuant to the trust, and Charity Y takes the State Z bonds.

REAL PROPERTY

Sample Question Number 3

Lisa owns' a five-story commercial building. On January 1, 1988, she leased the top floor to Tom for a five-year term at a rent of $500 a month. The lease was in writing and signed by both parties. It contained a restriction that the premises could be used only "as a dance studio and for no other purpose." It also provided: "Landlord shall not lease space in the building to any competitor of Tenant." The lease did not contain any express warranties or disclaimers.

Tom promptly moved in and began to operate a dance studio. In June 1988, he sold his dance studio business to Alice, one of his instructors, and assigned the lease to her. The assignment did not contain any express assumption or assignment of contract rights clauses.

In January 1989, a dance student fell through a floor board. When the board was replaced, it was discovered that, although the building met building code requirements, the floor was not strong enough for a dance studio.

In February, Lisa rented the basement to Charles who used it for aerobic exercise classes.

Alice wrote to Lisa demanding that Lisa have the floor strengthened and cancel the lease with Charles. Alice claimed that Charles was in competition with her. Lisa refused both requests. On July 1, 1989, Alice mailed the top floor key back to Lisa and moved out of the building. She has paid no rent since moving. Lisa has made all reasonable attempts to mitigate the loss.

Lisa has now sued both Tom and Alice for the rent due.
How should the court rule? Discuss.

Answer to Sample Question Number 3

Step One: Divide by legal issue *or* by party. Either:

83

1. Assignment
   a. Privity of Estate
   b. Privity of Contract
2. Implied Covenants
   a. Possession
   b. Quiet Enjoyment
   c. Habitability
3. Express Covenants
   a. To Pay Rent
   b. To Use Premises Only as a Dance Studio
   c. Not to Lease to Competitor
4. Frustration of Purpose
5. Remedies

OR:

Lisa v. Tom

Cause of Action—Rent Due

Defenses: Breach of Covenant Not to Lease to Competitor

Lisa v. Alice

Privity Issue
Cause of Action—Rent Due
Defenses: Breach of Implied and Express Covenants

Note: As a general rule, I prefer division of the question into legal issues rather than by party because it eliminates a lot of repetition, and thus, my sample answer here will follow that organization. However, either organization is acceptable.

Step Two: Begin with the issue

The first issue concerns whether and how the assignment affects Lisa's right to sue Tom and Alice.

Steps Three and Four: Break down into privity of estate and privity of contract; set out relevant law and apply it to the facts.

Assignment

Privity of Contract: Since Tom transferred all of his interests for the entire leasehold term, there was an assignment to Alice. This terminates Tom's privity of estate with Lisa, but he remains in privity of contract with her and thus remains obligated under the lease.

Privity of Estate: By virtue of the assignment, Alice falls into privity of estate with Lisa and is liable on all lease covenants that run with the land. Since the assignment did not contain an express assumption of any or all of the lease covenants, Alice is not in privity of contract with Lisa and is not bound by any covenants that do not run with the land.

Implied Covenants

There are three implied covenants in landlord/tenant leases.

a. *Covenant of Possession:* Since Tom took possession on the date promised, there is no problem with this covenant.

b. *Covenant of Quiet Enjoyment:* The law requires actual, partial actual, or constructive eviction to prove breach of this covenant. Constructive eviction is the substantial impairment of the use or enjoyment of the property.

Here, Tom and Alice can argue that the unsuitable floorboards and the lease to Charlie amount to constructive eviction. Coupled with an express covenant to use the premises only for a dance studio, the refusal to replace the unsuitable floor could amount to constructive eviction. Lisa's breach of the noncompetition clause by leasing the basement to an aerobics studio also probably amounts to a constructive eviction.

A constructive eviction entitles the tenant to either (i) sue for damages or (ii) abandon the premises within a reasonable time and terminate the lease. Here, Alice's six-month delay would probably not be considered reasonable, thus waiving her right to do so and leaving her with a suit for damages as her only remedy.

c. *Covenant of Habitability:* The covenant applies only to residential leases and therefore would not apply here.

Express Covenants

The lease contained three express covenants:

a. *Covenant to Pay Rent:* This covenant runs with the land. Thus, both Alice and Tom are liable under this covenant.

b. *Covenant to Use Premises Only as a Dance Studio:* This covenant also runs with the land. Alice did not breach this covenant; thus, it has no effect on her later failure to pay rent.

c. *Covenant Not to Lease to a Competitor:* This covenant also runs with the land. Intent for it to run is evidenced by the combination of no restriction against assignment and the express covenant pertaining to use as a dance studio. It would be foreseeable that the premises would be assigned to another dance class or teacher, who would need the promise of no competition.

The covenant runs to Alice as an assignee. The benefit touches and concerns the premises directly. However, this covenant is independent of the covenant to pay rent. The only relief due the tenant is damages.

Thus, none of the express covenants provides a basis for excusing nonpayment of rent.

Frustration of Purpose

A landlord owes a duty not to frustrate the tenant's purpose (here, of running a dance studio). The fact that the floor cannot support a dance studio would seem to frustrate Alice's purpose. However, since she did not vacate the premises for almost six months, and probably held classes during that time, it is arguable that there was no total frustration of Alice's purpose.

Remedies

Tom and Alice are jointly liable for rent for the full term of the lease.

A landlord has a choice of three remedies:

(1) Accept the surrender of the premises;

(2) Do nothing and sue for rent as it becomes due; and

(3) Rent the premises and sue tenant for any loss.

In some states, the landlord has a duty to mitigate damages.

TORTS

Sample Question Number 4

The four-story law school building of University, a private institution open to the public, had a defective elevator which frequently stopped between floors. The elevator had an alarm button which, if pressed, would ring a bell in the hallway and thus alert persons in the building to the fact that the elevator had stopped between floors with passengers inside it. The defective condition did not create any danger that the elevator might fall or otherwise physically injure any passenger.

Elco, an elevator maintenance company, had a contract with University to inspect, service, and maintain the elevator.

One night, Prof, a law teacher, and his secretary, Prim, had been working late in Prof's office on the fourth floor of the building on an overdue manuscript. They entered the elevator to leave at about 11:20 p.m. The official closing hour for the building was 11:00 p.m., but there were exit doors from the building which could be opened from the inside. Both Prof and Prim knew that the elevator frequently stopped between floors.

The elevator stopped between the second and third floors. Prof pressed the alarm button and the bell could be heard ringing in the hallway. Smith, a law student, was the only other person still in the building. He heard the alarm bell and realized that someone was trapped in the elevator. He thought this was very funny, and he deliberately did not call the campus maintenance staff.

Prof and Prim were not discovered and released until 8 a.m. the next day. Prof suffered from high blood pressure. This condition and his fright at being confined in the elevator caused him to sustain a heart attack after two hours in the elevator.

Prim suffered severe emotional distress due to being confined in the elevator and her fear that Prof was dying. She was subsequently embarrassed and humiliated by remarks of students who suggested that perhaps some amorous activity in the elevator might have caused Prof's heart attack. What rights do Prof and Prim each have against:

88

(a) Smith?

(b) Elco?

(c) University?

Answer to Sample Question Number 4

(a) *Prof & Prim v. Smith*

Smith was not an employee of University and bore no special relationship to Prof or Prim. He did not cause the plaintiffs' predicament and so was under no obligation to attempt a rescue or to call for help. Since no duty existed, none was breached, and no negligence action lies. Nor would a false imprisonment action lie, since he was under no legal duty to provide a means of escape for them.

(b) *Prof & Prim v. Elco*

Since it does not appear that Elco sold or installed the elevator, negligence is the only available tort theory. If Elco never began to perform its maintenance contract, its conduct would be called nonfeasance, and no tort action would lie. Even though the elevator often stopped between floors and needed a maintenance worker to start it again, this restarting did not go to the defect and may not be misfeasance.

If Elco committed misfeasance by trying to fix the defect, liability would arise for some of the harm caused by the defect. The physical harm suffered by plaintiffs was foreseeable; Elco's failure to do the repairs properly would be unreasonable and a breach of its duty. Prof's damages would be medical expenses and economic losses incurred as a result of the heart attack, plus pain and suffering. Prim suffered severe emotional distress from her confinement and fear. Even though she was in the "zone of danger," most states would bar recovery because she suffered purely emotional harm without any physical injury. In addition, her chances of getting damages for her embarrassment are small.

Elco could not reasonably have foreseen this type of harm coming from the remarks.

Elco may claim that plaintiffs were contributorily negligent in using the elevator after the building was closed, knowing of the defect. Even though it had an alarm bell, the likelihood that it would not be heard should have been considered. In comparative negligence states, there would be no complete bar in any event.

A similar defense is implied assumption of the risk. Both plaintiffs were aware that the elevator often stopped between floors and should have foreseen the possibility of delayed rescue late at night. On the other hand, because of Prof's high blood pressure, using the stairs from the fourth floor may not have been a reasonable alternative, calling into question whether the risk was "voluntarily assumed."

(c) *Prof & Prim v. University*

If University was negligent in hiring Elco, then University may be liable for Elco's negligence. However, nothing in the facts suggests that Elco was not an appropriate company to hire for elevator maintenance.

In any case, University may be vicariously liable for Elco's negligence even though Elco is an independent contractor, since the duties assumed by Elco were nondelegable because of public policy considerations. Maintaining elevators in the law school was part of University's duty to provide a safe place to work for employees, as well as its duty to keep public premises safe for visitors.

Damages and defenses are the same as discussed above.

CONTRACTS

Sample Question Number 5

On October 15, Coll, a collector of art, telephoned Art, a well-known painter, and said, "Last February I saw your painting of sunflowers. Is it still available and, if so, how much do you want for it?" Art responded, "You can have it for $25,000, and I can deliver it on November 1, but I want a clause in our contract stating that if either of us decides not to go through with the deal, the other party is entitled to $5,000." Coll replied, "You've got a deal. Draw up the papers and mail them to me."

The painting that Coll had in mind was entitled "Sunflowers." In July of that year, unknown to Coll, Art had painted another picture of sunflowers which he had entitled "Sunflowers II."

The next day, Art prepared, signed, dated, and mailed to Coll a document stating: "I hereby sell to Coll my sunflower painting for $26,000, the price to be paid and the painting to be picked up by Coll on November 1. In the event that either party fails to perform, it is agreed that, because of the difficulty of proving how much damages have been sustained by the nonbreaching party, the nonbreaching party shall be entitled to damages in the sum of $5,000."

Coll received the document on October 17. He telephoned Art that day and said, "I accept your offer and will pick up the painting on November 1." Coll did not sign the writing or return it to Art. The $26,000 figure in the writing was a typographical error made by Art's secretary. Neither Art nor Coll had noticed that the figure was $26,000, rather than the $25,000 they had specified in their October 15 telephone conversation.

On October 25, the directors of Museum expressed great interest in "Sunflowers." Flattered by their attention, Art delivered "Sunflowers" to Museum as a gift that same day.

On November 1, when Coll tendered $25,000, Art tendered to Coll the painting entitled "Sunflowers II." Coll refused to accept "Sunflowers II" and, at the same time, learned that "Sunflowers" had been donated to Museum.

91

What are Coll's rights and remedies, if any, against Art? Discuss. Against Museum? Discuss.

Answer to Sample Question Number 5

Chronology

10/15–Art orally offered to sell a painting for $25,000 to be delivered on November 1, with a $5,000 liquidated damages clause. Coll accepted.

10/16–Art prepared a written document which incorporated the latent ambiguity, changed the delivery terms, and misstated the price. Art signed it.

10/17–Coll accepted Art's written offer but did not sign or return it.

10/25–Art donated "Sunflowers" to Museum.

11/8–Coll tendered $25,000. Art tendered "Sunflowers II."

Coll's Rights Against Art

Formation of Contract: Coll would argue that during the October 15th phone call between him and Art a valid contract was formed for the sale of the painting "Sunflowers."

Art's response to Coll's question regarding how much he wanted for the Sunflowers painting appears to be a valid offer. The requisite present intent to contract may be implied from the language, "You can have it for $25,000." Additionally, the terms were clearly stated: the painting for $25,000; delivery on November 1.

Coll's response to Art's offer, "You've got a deal," appears to be a valid acceptance as it is an unequivocal assent to Art's terms.

Art may attempt, however, to assert several defenses to Coll's breach of contract claim.

First, Art may allege that there was an ambiguity involved since there were two paintings of sunflowers: "Sunflowers" and "Sunflowers II." However, if one party to an ambiguous contract is aware of the ambiguity while the other party is not, the contract will not fail but will be held enforceable according to the innocent party's interpretation.

The facts clearly indicate that Coll was unaware of the two paintings. On the other hand, it is a reasonable conclusion that Art was aware of the ambiguity. Furthermore, there probably was no ambiguity. During the phone conversation, Coll mentioned that he saw the painting in February. "Sunflowers II" was not painted until July. Therefore, Art would have known which sunflower painting Coll was referring to. Hence, the contract would not fail for ambiguity and would be enforceable for the painting that Coll referred to.

Second, Art may allege a Statute of Frauds defense since the painting constitutes goods worth over $500. A contract for the sale of goods for $500 or more is not enforceable unless its material terms are reflected in a writing signed by the party sought to be charged (*i.e.,* the party against whom enforcement is sought). Here, the paper signed by Art and sent to Coll would be a sufficient memorandum of the agreement to satisfy the Statute of Frauds, since it included the essential terms. The fact that Coll failed to sign and return the document does not affect its enforceability against Art (the party to be charged in this case).

Finally, Art may allege that he did not have an absolute duty to perform because the written memorandum required Coll to tender $26,000 rather than $25,000. However, the facts indicate that the figure was a typographical error by Art's secretary, and Coll will be able to show this despite the existence of the writing. Under the parol evidence rule, where the parties to an integrated agreement reduce it to writing, extrinsic evidence of prior or contemporaneous agreements is inadmissible to vary the terms of the writing. However, the rule does not preclude *reformation* of the agreement where an antecedent agreement was incorrectly reflected in the writing. Here, Coll may introduce evidence that the writing is in error and that the agreed figure was $25,000.

Art's failure to deliver the painting when Coll tendered the money on November 1 would therefore constitute a breach of the contract.

Remedy for Breach: Coll is not limited to the $5,000 set by the liquidated damages provision. A liquidated damages provision will be enforceable if actual damages were difficult to ascertain and the amount agreed upon was a reasonable forecast, at the time of formation of the contract, of compensatory damages in case of breach.

Here, although actual damages were difficult to determine because the painting was unique, there is no indication that the amount was a good-faith effort to forecast damages. Instead, it was proposed and accepted in the initial discussion as a ***forfeiture*** provision.

Because of the difficulty of establishing the amount of compensatory damages, Coll may either obtain restitution of the amount he has tendered to Art or seek specific performance of the contract. Coll can show that money damages are inadequate because the object of the contract (a painting) is unique, and that mutuality of remedy is present because he has tendered the money to Art. However, specific performance will not be available because the painting is no longer in Art's possession. Hence, the court will conclude that enforcement of the contract ***between the parties*** is not feasible.

Coll's Rights Against Museum

The purchase by a bona fide purchaser would cut off Coll's rights to the painting. Here, however, since the museum was a donee of the painting, it would not qualify as a bona fide purchaser. If Coll can show that Art made the transfer in fraud of Coll's rights, the court should impose a constructive trust on the painting. Museum, as constructive trustee, has as its sole duty the duty to convey the painting to Coll.

CIVIL PROCEDURE

Sample Question Number 6

Seler, a citizen of State S, and Byer, a citizen of State B, met in State B and signed a written contract by which Seler agreed to sell Whiteacre, located in State W, to Byer. The contract as written provided that the purchase price of Whiteacre was $85,000. Seler returned to State S and sent Byer a deed conveying good title to Whiteacre.

Byer did not send Seler any money, but brought an action against Seler for reformation of the contract to correct an alleged error in the contract price. Byer alleged that the agreed price was $35,000 and that the $85,000 figure in the contract was a typographical error. The action was brought in a federal district court in State B. Subject matter jurisdiction was based on diversity. Personal jurisdiction over Seler was based on service of process under State B's long-arm statute.

1. Seler moved to dismiss the action, alleging lack of both personal and subject matter jurisdiction. The motion was denied.

2. Seler then filed an answer asserting that the written contract accurately stated the agreed price. In addition, she counterclaimed for the $85,000 purchase price set forth in the contract and demanded a jury trial. Byer answered the counterclaim and moved to strike the demand for jury trial. The motion was denied.

3. Seler then served Byer with interrogatories demanding responses to the following questions: "(a) Have you had Whiteacre appraised? (b) If so, state by whom, state the appraised value or values, and attach copies of all written reports received from all appraisers." Over Byer's timely objections to the interrogatories, the court ordered disclosure only of the identity of appraisers and their appraised values.

4. At trial, Byer testified that the agreed price was $35,000 and that the $85,000 figure in the written contract was a typographical error. An appraiser testified on behalf of Byer that the value of Whiteacre when the contract was signed was at most $38,200. Byer rested his case. Seler testified that the agreed price was $85,000. The jury returned a verdict for Seler for $85,000 and judgment was

entered accordingly. Byer promptly made a "renewed motion for judgment as a matter of law" and in the alternative, a motion for new trial. The court granted the renewed motion for judgment as a matter of law. No other motions were made during or after trial.

(1) Did the court correctly rule on the motion to dismiss? Discuss.

(2) Did the court correctly rule on the motion to strike the demand for the jury trial? Discuss.

(3) Did the court correctly rule on the objections to the interrogatories? Discuss.

(4) Was the evidence admitted at trial such that the court was correct in granting the renewed motion for judgment as a matter of law? Discuss.

(5) What procedural argument or arguments should Seler have made in opposition to the renewed motion for a judgment as a matter of law? Discuss.

Answer to Sample Question Number 6

This essay raises five distinct questions. Each is examined in turn.

(1) *Did the court correctly rule on the motion to dismiss?*

Subject matter jurisdiction here is grounded on diversity of citizenship. The general diversity statute requires that the amount in controversy exceed $75,000, exclusive of costs and interests. Here Byer admits liability for $35,000 and seeks to reform a contract that provides for $85,000. Arguably, only the difference between these figures, or $50,000, is in issue here. On that interpretation, the amount of controversy does not exceed

$75,000, and the suit should have been dismissed for lack of subject matter jurisdiction. On balance, this seems the correct resolution.

On another view, however, Byer is seeking to avoid contractual liability for $85,000. If Byer loses, Byer will owe Seler that amount. On this interpretation, more than $75,000 is in issue, and subject matter jurisdiction exists. However, the fact that Seler counterclaimed for $85,000 does not matter, as the claim stated in the *complaint* is dispositive.

Personal jurisdiction exists here if State B's long-arm statute so provides. Under the Federal Rules of Civil Procedure, personal jurisdiction in this action depends on state law. If state law has been complied with, the only remaining question is whether the Federal Constitution permits State B to assert in personam jurisdiction over Seler on these facts. The answer is "yes." Seler met Byer in State B and signed the contract there. The forum state thus has "minimum contacts" with Seler such that it is not inconsistent with traditional notions of fair play and substantial justice to sue Seler in State B on a contract made there. By engaging in business activities in State B, Seler has purposely availed herself of the benefits of the laws of that state and become subject to suit there, at least for actions arising out of her conduct there.

(2) Did the court correctly deny the motion to strike the demand for jury trial?

Seler's right to a jury trial in federal court is governed by the Seventh Amendment. Under that provision Seler is entitled to demand a trial by jury on factual legal issues determinative of the counterclaim, and this is true regardless of the fact that Byer's original suit for contract reformation was equitable in nature.

The issue is, therefore, whether Seler's counterclaim is legal or equitable in nature. Seler has demanded $85,000, which is the contract price of the land. If this counterclaim is viewed as an action for damages, then it is legal in nature, and Seler is entitled to demand jury trial. It may be, however, that Seler's counterclaim is not fairly characterized as an action for damages, which would lead only to recovery of the difference between the contract price and the value of the land. Instead, Seler seeks to recover the contract price of $85,000. In essence, Seler seeks specific performance of the contract, and specific performance is an equitable remedy. On that analysis, the court improperly denied the motion to strike the demand for jury trial.

(3) Did the court correctly rule on the objections to the interrogatories?

As a threshold matter, the interrogatories must meet the test of relevance. One could argue that the appraised value of the land is irrelevant to the dispute over whether the contract contained a typographical error, but that argument seems mistaken. Surely, the appraised value of the land would be logically relevant to determining what the parties to the contract in fact intended. That relevance would rest on the assumption that the intended contract price would likely bear some rough relation to appraised value.

Additionally, there may be problems with the work product doctrine. This doctrine provides a qualified immunity against discovery for documents prepared in anticipation of litigation by or for another party or his or her representative. If these appraisals were not sought in anticipation of litigation, they should be discoverable in the ordinary course. If they were sought in anticipation of litigation, the appraisals will be discoverable only if Byer intends to use them by calling the appraisers as expert witnesses at trial. Experts who are to be called at trial must be identified and their reports revealed. Experts who are not to be called at trial need not be so identified, and their reports are ordinarily not discoverable.

(4) Was the evidence admitted at trial such that the court was correct in granting the renewed motion for judgment as a matter of law?

A renewed motion for judgment as a matter of law is proper only where the evidence would permit no reasonable trier of fact to find for the party opposing the motion. Here the evidence in Byer's favor is not so overwhelming. Byer and Seler have given differing accounts of the intended transaction. This raises a straightforward issue of witness credibility, which the jurors are entitled to assess for themselves. Byer's testimony is corroborated in a minor way by the appraiser's testimony that the land was worth no more than $38,200. That opinion, however, scarcely precludes the possibility that the agreed price was in fact $85,000. Seler's testimony to that effect is confirmed by the written contract. Thus, granting Byer's motion was improper.

(5) *What procedural argument(s) should Seler have made in opposition to the renewed motion for judgment as a matter of law?*

A prerequisite to a renewed motion for a judgment as a matter of law is a motion for a judgment as a matter of law at the close of all the evidence. If, as appears, Byer failed make such a motion at the close of all the evidence, Byer is precluded from subsequently renewing the motion.

NOTES

R/BRI of Alabama
0 Church Street, Suite 102
hville, Tennessee 37203
0) 922-7274

R/BRI of Alaska
0 E. Madison Street, Suite 321
ttle, Washington 98112
6) 329-5250

R/BRI of Arizona
East University, Suite 207
npe, Arizona 85281
0) 929-0190

R/BRI of Arkansas
0 Church Street, Suite 102
hville, Tennessee 37203
8) 922-7274

R/BRI of California
0 Motor Avenue, Suite 200
Angeles, California 90034
0) 995-5227

R/BRI of Colorado
orado Bar Refreshern, Inc.
7 East Evans Avenue, Unit #1
ver, Colorado 80222
3) 757-5575

R/BRI of Connecticut
t. James Avenue, Suite 820
ton, Massachusetts 02116
0) 866-7277

R/BRI of Delaware
ener Delaware Bar Review
1 Concord Pike/P.O. Box 7474
nington, Delaware 19803
2) 477-2087

R/BRI of Washington, D.C.
0 18th Street, N.W., Lower Level
hington, D.C. 20036
0) 876-3086

R/BRI of Florida
0-28 Sharer Road
ahassee, Florida 32312
0) 950-7277

R/BRI of Georgia
West Broad Street
ourn, Georgia 30213
0) 360-7277

R/BRI of Hawaii
Box 441
olulu, Hawaii 96809
8) 537-2556

R/BRI of Idaho
ast University, Suite 207
pe, Arizona 85281
0) 729-0190

BAR/BRI of Illinois
111 W. Jackson Boulevard, 7th Floor
Chicago, Illinois 60604
(800) 621-0498

BAR/BRI of Indiana
46998 Magellan Drive, Suite 200
Wixom, Michigan 48393
(800) 937-2778

BAR/BRI of Iowa
Iowa Bar Association
521 East Locust Street, 3rd Floor
Des Moines, Iowa 50309
(515) 243-3179

BAR/BRI of Kansas
46998 Magellan Drive, Suite 200
Wixom, Michigan 48393
(800) 937-2778

BAR/BRI of Kentucky
Kentucky Law Review Institute, Inc.
11603 Shelbyville Road, Units 7&8
Louisville, Kentucky 40243
(800) 320-7789

BAR/BRI of Louisiana
1415 Fannin, Suite 250
Houston, Texas 77002
(800) 392-5441

BAR/BRI of Maine
31 St. James Avenue, Suite 820
Boston, Massachusetts 02116
(800) 866-7277

BAR/BRI of Maryland
1150 18th Street, N.W., Lower Level
Washington, D.C. 20036
(800) 876-3086

Modern Bar Review
1501 Sulgrave Avenue, Suite 201
Baltimore, Maryland 21209
(888) 385-4922

BAR/BRI of Massachusetts
31 St. James Avenue, Suite 820
Boston, Massachusetts 02116
(800) 866-7277

BAR/BRI of Michigan
46998 Magellan Drive, Suite 200
Wixom, Michigan 48393
(800) 937-2778

BAR/BRI of Minnesota
701 Fourth Avenue South
Suite 1710
Minneapolis, Minnesota 55415
(800) 328-4444

BAR/BRI of Mississippi
P.O. Box 56
Ridgeland, Mississippi 39158
(601) 856-8388

BAR/BRI of Missouri
46998 Magellan Drive, Suite 200
Wixom, Michigan 48393
(800) 937-2778

BAR/BRI of Montana
330 Blue Heron Lane
Missoula, Montana 59804
(406) 542-2595

BAR/BRI of Nebraska
2810-28 Sharer Road
Tallahassee, Florida 32312
(800) 410-7277

BAR/BRI of Nevada
20 East University, Suite 207
Tempe, Arizona 85281
(800) 729-0190

BAR/BRI of New Hampshire
31 St. James Avenue, Suite 820
Boston, Massachusetts 02116
(617) 695-9955

BAR/BRI of New Jersey
1500 Broadway
New York, New York 10036
(800) 472-8899

BAR/BRI of New Mexico
5612 Cometa Ct., NE
Albuquerque, New Mexico 87110
(505) 888-3040

BAR/BRI of New York
1500 Broadway
New York, New York 10036
(800) 472-8899

BAR/BRI of North Carolina
200 Meredith Drive, Suite 104
Durham, North Carolina 27713
(800) 300-1822

BAR/BRI of North Dakota
701 Fourth Avenue South, Suite 1710
Minneapolis, Minnesota 55415
(800) 328-4444

BAR/BRI of Ohio
Bank One Center
600 Superior Avenue, Suite 2550
Cleveland, Ohio 44114
(800) 937-2778

BAR/BRI of Oklahoma
1415 Fannin, Suite 250
Houston, Texas 77002
(800) 392-5441

BAR/BRI of Oregon
4020 E. Madison Street, Suite 321
Seattle, Washington 98122
(206) 329-5250

BAR/BRI of Pennsylvania
1800 JFK Boulevard, Suite 500
Philadelphia, Pennsylvania 19103
(800) 452-7277

BAR/BRI of Rhode Island
31 St. James Avenue, Suite 820
Boston, Massachusetts 02116
(800) 866-7277

BAR/BRI of South Carolina
South Carolina Bar Review
P.O. Box 11424
Columbia, South Carolina 29211
(803) 252-3971

BAR/BRI of South Dakota
111 W. Jackson Boulevard, 7th Floor
Chicago, Illinois 60604
(800) 621-0498

BAR/BRI of Tennessee
1900 Church Street, Suite 102
Nashville, Tennessee 37203
(800) 738-8529

BAR/BRI of Texas
1415 Fannin, Suite 250
Houston, Texas 77002
(800) 392-5441

BAR/BRI of Utah
20 East University Drive, Suite 207
Tempe, Arizona 85281
(800) 729-0190

BAR/BRI of Vermont
31 St. James Avenue, Suite 820
Boston, Massachusetts 02116
(800) 866-7277

BAR/BRI of Virginia
1150 18th Street, N.W., Lower Level
Washington, D.C. 20036
(800) 876-3086

BAR/BRI of Washington
4020 E. Madison Street, Suite 321
Seattle, Washington 98112
(206) 329-5250

BAR/BRI of West Virginia
440 Rotary Street
Morgantown, West Virginia 26505
(888) 222-7274

BAR/BRI of Wisconsin
950 Auburn Court
Brookfield, Wisconsin 53045
(262) 792-9165

BAR/BRI of Wyoming
Summit Bar Review
P.O. Box 1710
Laramie, Wyoming 82073
(307) 742-6644

Last year over 23,000 students used BAR/BRI to prepare for first year exams.

There's a good reason why.

FIRST YEAR REVIEW

Our Students Pass!

If You're Not Using Us, You're Working Too Hard.

lbert Law Summaries are the best selling outlines in the country, and have set the standard for excellence ice they were first introduced more than thirty-five years ago. It's Gilbert's unique combination of features at makes it the one study aid you'll turn to for all your study needs.

BOOKS

tle	Keyed To	Price
counting & Finance		
or Lawyers	Evans	$19.95
ministrative Law	Asimow	$20.95
ency & Partnership	Conviser	$17.95
titrust	Jorde, Lemley, Mnookin	$18.95
kruptcy	Waxman	$21.95
ril Procedure	Marcus, Rowe	$22.95
mmercial Paper &		
ayment Law	Whaley	$19.95
mmunity Property	Reppy	$18.95
iflict of Laws	Kay	$20.95
nstitutional Law	Choper	$21.95
ntracts	Eisenberg	$21.95
rporations	Choper, Eisenberg	$21.95
minal Law	Dix	$20.95
minal Procedure	Marcus, Whitebread	$20.95
ate & Gift Tax	McCord	$20.95
dence	Waltz, Park	$22.95

BOOKS

Title	Keyed To	Price
Federal Courts	Fletcher	$21.95
Future Interests	Dukeminier	$19.95
Income Tax I (Individual)	Asimow	$21.95
Income Tax II (Partnerships,		
Corporations, Trusts)	Asimow	$19.95
Labor Law	Gelhaus, Oldham	$19.95
Legal Ethics	Morgan	$20.95
Legal Research, Writing &		
Analysis	Honigsberg	$17.95
Personal Property	Gilbert	$14.95
Property	Dukeminier	$22.95
Remedies	Bauman	$22.95
Sales & Lease of Goods	Whaley	$19.95
Secured Transactions	Whaley	$18.95
Securities Regulation	Schaumann	$22.95
Torts	Franklin	$22.95
Trusts	Halbach	$20.95
Wills	Johanson	$21.95

Employment Guides

- **America's Greatest Places to Work with a Law Degree** (Kimm Alayne Walton, J.D.) $24.95

- **The Best of the Job Goddess: Phenomenal Job Search Advice from the Country's Most Popular Legal Job Search Columnist** (Kimm Alayne Walton, J.D.) $14.95

- **Behind the Bench: The Guide to Judicial Clerkships** (Debra M. Strauss, J.D.) $21.95

- **Guerrilla Tactics for Getting the Legal Job of Your Dreams—Regardless of Your Grades, Your School, or Your Work Experience!** (Kimm Alayne Walton, J.D.) $24.95

- **The Official Guide to Legal Specialties: An Insider's Guide to Every Major Practice Area** (Lisa L. Abrams, J.D.) $19.95

- **Proceed with Caution: A Diary of a First Year at One of America's Most Prestigious Law Firms** (William Keates, J.D.) $17.95

- **What Law School Doesn't Teach You...But You Really Need to Know! Expert Tips & Strategies for Making Your Legal Career a Huge Success.** (Kimm Alayne Walton, J.D.) $24.95